W9-AXK-803

PRAISE FOR *LAUNCH!*

"Real-life principles that actually work!"
—FRANK SHANKWITZ, founder, The Make-A-Wish Foundation

"*Launch!* is a must read and truly impactful book for any entrepreneur."
—GENE LANDRUM, president and creative force,
Chuck E. Cheese, Entrepreneur Hall of Fame

"Scott Duffy expertly guides you through what it takes to launch a new business—from the deep personal sacrifices you make for a project you wholeheartedly believe in to the incredible high you get when your mission becomes a success. *Launch!* is an invaluable companion with real-life examples for anyone willing to dream big, break barriers, and turn their idea into reality."
—KRISTI AND ANDY FUNK, founders,
Pink Lotus Breast Center

"Scott is one of the most dynamic, positive, and creative people I have had the good fortune to know. Scott is a great leader in all areas of life. I'm honored to be in his corner."
—DOUG BRIGNOLE, Mr. Universe, Mr. America, author, speaker

"This book isn't just about launching—it's about setting the stage to build better companies. It's a must read."
—DENA COOK, CEO, Brew Media Relations

"In *Launch!*, Scott's ability to connect with entrepreneurs is unparalleled. His passion and genuine drive to help others grow is infectious."
—NICOLE HURD, founder,
National College Advising Corps.

"It's about time somebody wrote a book about launching new ventures that doesn't just look at the business side of entrepreneurship, but at the human side as well! Scott Duffy shows how you, too, can build a stronger, more successful business by paying attention to all parts of your life as you launch and grow your business."
—MICHELLE PATTERSON, executive director,
Women Network Foundation and The CA Women's Conference

"*Launch!* shows us how the right attitude, the right focus, and the right idea need to come together for a successful launch."
—CHRIS FRALIC, partner, First Round Capital

"What makes *Launch!* such a fun and compelling read is Scott's personal experiences launching new ventures. He's learned the lessons of a successful launch through real-world experience and proves how you, too, can take your big idea to market."
—KALIKA YAP, CEO, Citrus Studios

"Scott is an incredible entrepreneur who will show you the way to success. He will inspire you through your successful *Launch!*"
—RON KLEIN, inventor of the credit card magnetic strip verification system, Multiple Listing Service, business consultant, problem solver

"I wish I had had this book when I was launching my company. Scott's blend of business smarts, useful takeaways, and empathy is much needed in today's fast-start environment."
—LORI TAYLOR, founder, REV Media Marketing

"Launching a new product or service is incredibly tough—but you're not alone. Scott Duffy is here to guide you through the tough, crucial, exhilarating first days of the launch, with tips, tricks, and tools that will help you get off to the right start."
—GERRY MORTON, president and CEO, Energy First

"In *Launch!* Scott Duffy keeps all the priorities—family, community, business—in a positive balance. He is a value-added adviser to entrepreneurs and his advice is key to a successful business and launch."
—DEMETRIOS A. BOUTRIS, California Corporations commissioner (ret.)

"As I was finishing my master's in exercise science, I planned on building my own coaching business in the health and fitness world. The very first person I reached out to was Scott Duffy. Scott talked to me about the successes of entrepreneurs and the fails of entrepreneurs. He made me think about what I needed to do in the health and fitness world, by '*Launch!*-ing' my brand, my expertise, and my knowledge. This book is for people who are starting a business from scratch to people who may need to tweak their

business to make it a success. I promise you, with Scott's brand, expertise, and knowledge . . . you will *not* be disappointed."
—Jennifer Rulon, M.S., USA Triathlon Level I Coach

"Scott Dufffy knows what it's like to launch a new company from the ground up. In his book *Launch!,* he shares the wealth of his experiences with us—and shows us how anyone can take their big idea to market quickly, efficiently, and successfully."
—Jason Port, investor,
strategist, founding investor in Quirky.com

"Scott Duffy has condensed years of real-world business experience into an easy-to-use playbook. Packed with relevant real-world advice you can use today. Essential reading for anyone looking to start a business or launch a new product within an existing business."
–Gene Lim, Global Strategic Alliances,
Entrepreneurs Organization, and CEO MAV12

"Scott Duffy's guide to launching new businesses is a must read: *Launch!* is snappy, cutting edge, entertaining, and with useful take-aways on every page. Let me put it this way, it's *awesome* and it's now required reading for everyone on my boards of my businesses!"
—Erik "Mr. Awesome" Swanson,
Universal Seminars and The Habitude Warrior

"Scott is the consummate visionary and a born leader. He is a passionate, relentless serial entrepreneur who will make many more dreams reality."
—Drew Boyles, president,
Entrepreneurs' Organization–Los Angeles

LAUNCH!

LAUNCH!

THE CRITICAL 90 DAYS FROM IDEA TO MARKET

SCOTT DUFFY

PORTFOLIO / PENGUIN

PORTFOLIO / PENGUIN

Published by the Penguin Group
Penguin Group (USA) LLC
375 Hudson Street
New York, New York 10014

USA | Canada | UK | Ireland | Australia | New Zealand | India | South Africa | China
penguin.com
A Penguin Random House Company

First published by Portfolio / Penguin, a member of Penguin Group (USA) LLC, 2014

LIBRARY OF CONGRESS CATALOGING-IN-PUBLICATION DATA
Duffy, Scott.
Launch! : the critical 90 days from idea to market / Scott Duffy.
pages cm
Includes index.
ISBN 978-1-59184-606-2
1. Entrepreneurship.   2. New business enterprises.   3. New products.   I. Title.
HB615.D837 2013
658.1'1—dc23
2013039077

Printed in the United States of America
10 9 8 7 6 5 4 3 2 1

Set in Sabon LT Std
Designed by E. J. Strongin, Neuwirth & Associates, Inc.

To Rachel

Love at first sight, love of my life

and

To Lily and Lexi

I am so proud to be your dad

CONTENTS

STAGE I.

The Prelaunch Checklist: Thirty Days to Prepare

STAGE II.

Fueling the Tank: Thirty Days to Assemble Your Resources

STAGE III.

Countdown and Blastoff: The First Thirty Days of Business

PREFACE

Over 97 percent of a rocket's fuel is used during the first three feet of its launch. The same is true when launching a new business, product, or service.

The first few steps are absolutely critical. But this is where most entrepreneurs make their biggest mistakes—and set themselves off on a path to failure.

Launch! The Critical Ninety Days from Idea to Market is a flight plan for entrepreneurs and managers within large organizations who aim to get their new business or product off the ground successfully. It is a philosophical and systematic approach for turning your passion into a thriving venture while mitigating risk every step of the way.

Why ninety days? Because that's all the time you have. Today your competition is faster, more agile, and better equipped. In the modern business era, speed is like gold. It's the most valuable currency at your disposal. In 1996 I was working at a consumer Internet start-up in Silicon Valley. At launch we had just one competitor. In sixty days we had seventeen competitors. In ninety days we had almost one hundred. And that was more than fifteen years ago, when things moved at a snail's pace! The marketplace has only gotten more crowded.

Speed also protects you. With a short time frame, you put fewer dollars at risk and streamline your focus. In ninety days you will be able to take your idea, go to market, get valuable feedback, and make well-informed decisions about what to do next—all without breaking the bank.

I believe it's not only possible but also critical to launch a new business, product, or service in such a short time, and over the years I've developed a systematic approach that divides launching into three phases.

In *"Stage I: The Prelaunch Checklist,"* the goal is simple: to protect what is most important: you! That means we'll strategize on getting your house in order and limiting your personal risk, so if things do not work out as planned, you can bounce right back.

"Stage II: Fueling the Tank" is the process of assembling your resources. Here we'll look at pulling together your plan, your team, your capital, and other key business resources that will put you in the best position to execute successfully.

"Stage III: Countdown and Blastoff" takes your big idea to market. In this section we'll nail down all the critical aspects of targeting your market specifically and launching your product successfully around day sixty. This includes developing partnerships, distribution channels, customer-engagement strategies, marketing and public-relations efforts, sales initiatives, and customer support. With each step, I will provide you with a plan for anticipating what comes next and managing through problems in a way that turns them into opportunities.

The lessons in this book are not academic but are based on my personal experience as an entrepreneur and business leader. I started my career working in the business and personal-development training industry before falling in love with technology. In the midnineties I moved to Silicon Valley and spent the next fifteen years helping to launch and grow companies from a very early stage. Many companies I was a part of became big brands like CBS Sportsline, NBC Internet, FOXSports.com, and Virgin Charter. There were other ventures along the way. Some have been big successes while others have been big failures. The lessons from each experience were invaluable, and I'll share them with you in this book.

In the last twenty years I've also benefited from working for some of the greatest entrepreneurs and innovators of our time, including Richard Branson and Tony Robbins. In the following pages you'll hear stories about how they, along with others, such as Spanx inventor Sara Blakely and Starbucks CEO Howard Schultz, dealt with the challenges of launching.

You may ask, *What could I possibly have in common with these people?* The answer is: *everything.* They started with a vision, just like you. They backed it up with passion and perseverance. They have all been through the ups and downs that come along with being an entrepreneur or launching a new initiative inside a big organization. They combined hard work with hard-learned lessons to create successful ventures with lasting impact—just as you will do.

I am absolutely committed to doing whatever I can to help you launch your big idea to the world and make your dreams come true. I have set up a Web site at www.scottduffy.com with free tools and video-based lessons to provide you with additional inspiration and support. I encourage you to visit it.

In return, I ask just one thing. For the next ninety days, suspend any doubts or disbelief about your ability to launch successfully. Know that you can be more, do more, and have more than you ever thought possible. If you follow the steps in this book and execute like crazy, in the next ninety days you'll begin to make your dreams come true.

Let's get ready to launch.

INTRODUCTION

The Entrepreneur Economy

I am building a fire, and every day I train, I add more fuel. At just the right moment, I light the match.

—MIA HAMM

There has never been a better time to be an entrepreneur. Today there are more businesses, products, and services being launched than at any time in history. Increased competition and faster-moving product and business cycles are contributing factors.

This scares the hell out of big business.

Ten years ago the barriers to launching and building a successful company were often too high for small entrepreneurs. As a result, a big company's competition was primarily limited to other big companies. Managers could literally look outside their windows and see their competition. They knew each other well, could spot each other's strengths and weaknesses, and could compete effectively with each other. But those days are over.

In the new entrepreneur economy, the low barrier to entry for new products and services has created fierce competition on every front. The modern-day entrepreneur, who is either using his existing venture to bring new products to market or launching a new business from the ground up, moves more quickly than big companies and can often position himself to meet customer needs better, faster, and cheaper. To make things even more difficult for big businesses, it's not just one entrepreneur they need to watch out for. There are literally millions of entrepreneurs, armed with laptops, smart phones, and free tools from the Internet, nibbling at their feet. Competition now comes from anywhere and everywhere.

These new entrepreneurs are also more motivated than at any time before. Many have recovered from the global collapse of 2008 by adapting their business practices to the economic conditions and by leveraging all available resources. Today rising companies run leaner, stronger, and more efficiently and generate greater profits. Others, hurt by the crash of 2008, may have lost their savings or jobs so they've had to reinvent themselves in ways they never imagined. Now that they are getting back on their feet, these entrepreneurs are hungrier and driven by real purpose. They move fast because they have to; they move with purpose because they know the consequences of not doing so. They're also fearless and are going after big businesses and successfully stealing their market share, one customer at a time.

Big companies have a big problem in this new landscape: Most have bloated cultures that move too slowly to launch fast and compete against this new breed of entrepreneurs. While ninety days is enough time for an entrepreneur to launch a new business, product, or service, it takes most big businesses ninety days to make a decision on whether or not to even *get in the game*. Once they decide to compete, it might take them another nine hundred days to actually do it.

On the other hand, many entrepreneurs, despite their potential for speed and agility, still rely on a combination of passion (which can take you only so far) and outdated strategies that are out of sync with best practices of the new economy. That's where this book comes in, bridging that gap between the old approach and what it really takes to generate success in this economic era. By applying the lessons in this book, you can set yourself up to be in the best starting position to launch and come out head and shoulders above the competition.

The old notion of an entrepreneur brought to mind people like Richard Branson, Donald Trump, and others who appeared to take gigantic risks, putting everything they had both personally and professionally on the line. Not all entrepreneurs can think of themselves in this light, nor is it responsible for them to take on that much risk.

But today everyone is an entrepreneur. It's not about building the next Virgin or Google or Facebook. It's about planting a flag. Transforming what you are passionate about, what you are good at, into a responsible, moneymaking venture that benefits others in the process.

Launch! is a handbook for entrepreneurs on how to think big, take on any size competitor—and eat their lunch. I want to help you become a modern-day business version of David, where as a small and agile entrepreneur, you can defeat the big corporate Goliath. This is your opportunity. Seize it.

Ink Versus the Mac

I've been called a "serial entrepreneur." Whatever the name caller's intention, I love the expression. It speaks to my history as well as my passion.

At a very early age, my family exposed me to business. For fifty years, all the men on my father's side—my father, my grandfather, back to my great-grandfather—ran a printing and engraving shop. One of the things I remember most clearly about my childhood was my father, like all the good tradesmen, coming home with the distinctive smell of ink on his hands and clothes.

Back then, printing and engraving was a very manual business. Skilled craftsmen spent years as apprentices, learning their trade. Photographers, engravers, and dot etchers pooled their skills, working with advertising agencies to take photos and create artwork that they melded into advertisements, outdoor billboards, and all sorts of printed materials. Their industry played a vital role in marketing and held a well-recognized place in society. My family made money, the skilled employees were paid well, and everybody took pride in the work they did. Then computer technology turned the business on its head.

I have always straddled the digital divide. The year after I finished grammar school, typing became a mandatory class. The year after I graduated from high school, computers became a fixture in the classroom. As a freshman in college, I bought an electronic typewriter—and I really thought it rocked—but was soon introduced to an even more game-changing piece of technology. Sophomore year, my roommate arrived carrying a newfangled computer all his own. He called it a "Mac." That desktop machine may have been just one tool—by today's standards a primitive one—but it meant he was a light-year ahead of where I was. Being able to use a word processor to do your homework? *Wow!*

When the first Apple Macintosh came to the printing business, the process of producing an advertisement changed forever. Tradesmen on both sides of the table, the advertising agencies and the service providers, had much invested in the old way of doing things, including skills they had developed over a lifetime. They had a lot to lose from change, so they didn't learn new skills or change the way they did business overnight. But even that rudimentary computer created a weird energy in the shop when it was first installed. It was a mystical moment, almost as if everyone had suddenly seen the future. To complicate matters, that Mac was literally placed right in the middle of the office. You couldn't avoid it. Some of the workers in the shop embraced it while others tried to pretend it was not there.

The guys on the floor may have had some sixth sense that, soon enough, the job of the craftsman, working with paper, rulers, and glue, would become obsolete. I got the feeling that people walked around on tiptoes in hopes that they could delay the waking of that big elephant in the room for another day or week. That didn't work, of course. With the Mac, processes that had taken three men three days by the old manual routine could be completed by one man in three hours. Prep jobs could be done for a fraction of what they had cost a year or two earlier. The cost of making corrections or changes to a printed piece dropped significantly. As customers learned of these efficiencies, the savvy ones insisted that those savings be passed on to them. If you were really paying attention, you could tell that the smell of ink in the room had begun to fade.

The Mac initiated the change, but the Internet accelerated it. Pretty soon nobody needed to drive around delivering printing proofs to their customers. Knocking on doors and pursuing sales leads the old way was also finished. Despite decades of stability, the introduction of new technology disrupted the industry rapidly. Many businesses vanished, along with the three-martini lunch.

This was a big lesson for me at an early age. The good men I grew up with had a lot to lose by not adapting. Many were afraid to change and were afraid of the unknown. But the ones who embraced change, who recognized that technology could propel them forward, learned to use the Macs (or other technologies) and thrived. Some even opened up new shops where they did the same work—only better, faster, and cheaper. They found new pride in their work. Those who refused to change? Well, some of them became unemployable.

The whole experience made one thing crystal clear: that you have to live your life through the windshield, not through the rearview mirror.

On a Mexican Highway

Another huge lesson for my future business life was the importance of adaptability. I was first exposed to the need to adapt while attending the University of San Diego. There I started a business, played sports, and lived on the beach, generally having the time of my life. After midterm exams in the fall of 1989, following tradition, a group of friends and I packed up our cars and headed on a ten-hour drive south to the beaches of San Felipe, Mexico. I thought I was bound for fun in the sun and a great time with friends.

And then, in a heartbeat, everything changed.

We were several miles south of the border, traveling on a two-lane highway. The landscape was surreal. There was nothing but desert on both sides of the road as far as one could see.

Suddenly, a truck pulled out right in front of us. There was no time to stop, and we hit it squarely, going about seventy-five miles per hour. Sitting in the passenger seat, I was tossed about like a beanbag. All four of us in the car were injured. The guys in the truck we hit just drove off and left us there, alone in the desert, bleeding and in pain.

It was the *worst* day of my life.

How many times in your life have you been going down a road, doing everything right? Your timing was perfect. You had a solid plan and team in place. You executed flawlessly. Then, out of no-where, something unexpected knocked you off course. Think about those events in your life where the ground just moved underneath your feet, when everything you had done up to that point, everything you had accomplished, had to be thrown out. You had to start over, right?

That's exactly what happened to me.

The accident was bad, the recuperation no better. I ended up at the Scripps Clinic in La Jolla with significant head injuries, including two brain hemorrhages, and a long road to recovery. I couldn't read without headaches or nausea, and I couldn't even bear to watch TV. Studying was out of the question, so I was forced to stop going to class and effectively dropped out of school.

Despite having lost so much in that accident, I developed a habit in those weeks and months that changed my life forever. I started listening to motivational books on tape. The first program I listened to was from Tony Robbins, and throughout my recovery I got my hands on others, including audiobooks from Jim Rohn, Brian Tracy, Denis Waitley, and Zig Ziglar. I listened to these audiobooks all day, every day. I was inspired by the idea that if you have the desire and are willing to make a commitment to follow through and take action, you can achieve virtually anything you want in life. All the resources you need to get started are within you now or within your reach.

Sometimes my head hurt so much that I had to keep the volume really low on the tapes, so low that I could barely hear the speaker. But I absorbed everything they had to teach me. I also learned that many of these trainers were based in San Diego. I decided that, when I got better, I would go back to school and apply for an internship with one of them. It would be my motivation for powering through my recovery. As my first target, I decided to seek out Tony Robbins.

Due to the early success of his infomercials, Tony was on his way to becoming a household name. I knew I'd have to do something big to get his attention, something to stand out. I thought it through and finally I came up with an idea.

Tony is a big guy, six feet, seven inches tall. So I got a very tall cardboard box, filled it with packing material, and enclosed in it my résumé and items representing all his biggest accomplishments (a copy of his book, one of his tapes, a flyer for a live event, a picture of Tony and his wife I found in a magazine). I also enclosed a flyer that asked, "How can Robbins Research benefit with Scott Duffy as a member of its team?" By way of answering the question, I listed my traits and all he would gain by hiring me as an intern. I figured because the box was so big he would engage with it, curious to see what was inside. If I was lucky, he'd remember me. I didn't want to blend in (in a competitive business, neither can you). Then I waited, hoping a good thing would happen.

Well, it did. My package got the reaction I'd hoped for and I got a call from Michael "Hutch" Hutchison, who was leading Tony's team. He invited me to come in for an interview. Two more interviews followed. During the third, Hutch asked me to stand in front of the room as if I were facing a big audience and rapidly fired questions at me. After about twenty minutes he left the room, leaving me alone. The minutes ticked by. I waited patiently, just thinking how awesome it would be to work with them. Finally, after an hour had passed, Hutch came in and said he had forgotten I was still in the office . . . but I was hired! Not as an intern, either, but as a full-time employee.

My work for Tony Robbins in the coming months took me on the road, often traveling from city to city promoting his live events, most notably "Power to Influence," one of his first business programs. I would go into offices and deliver a part of the program to a group of employees, selling them the value of seeing Robbins live. I gave these talks up to five times a day. I was immersed in the Robbins way of thinking; I must have seen him teach ten courses over the next year. Traveling the country, I soaked up his wisdom and shared it with others. Working with his team helped me recover and propelled my life in a whole new direction.

When I got started working for Robbins Research I was twenty-one years old. I spoke to over two hundred companies, from FedEx to Mary Kay Cosmetics. I learned to look at the world differently, not only through Tony's teaching but also through the teaching of others in the industry and the colleagues I came to know along the way. I met men and women who have remained among my best friends to this day. I had incredible experiences but, most important, I was exposed every day to people who had overcome huge obstacles and looked at them as growth opportunities.

This shifted my mind-set. It taught me the power of controlling your focus both personally and professionally. It taught me that, no matter how bad a situation may seem in the moment, we have the ability to learn from it and assign new meaning that moves us closer to our goals. Mastering this skill would have a tremendous impact on my life and my business. It also opened my mind up to a real sense of what is possible.

I remember having lunch with Tony in Seattle with our team. I opened up to him about the accident I had had in Mexico and how terrible the experience had been. I told him I had felt like I had to throw everything away and relaunch. But so much good had come out it: new experiences, a more powerful way of thinking, a sense of unlimited possibility, a really solid foundation for business going forward, and great new friends.

His response really put the experience in perspective. "You have good days and bad days," he said. "But you don't know which is which until someday way down the line, because you don't know what you will make of that experience."

Over the years I've found this to be one of the most important lessons I have learned in life and business. What has happened to you in the past matters much less than what you learned *and* how you apply each lesson going forward.

As an entrepreneur, you too can overcome your wreckage. Everyone has a story and has experienced setbacks in his or her life. It could be that you had a business that failed or that you were laid off. Maybe you were hurt financially, filed for bankruptcy, or lost a house. Perhaps you suffered an accident or were in poor health or had your heart broken. Just know it's not the experience; it's what you do with the experience. Remember, nothing in life has any meaning other than the meaning you give it. One of the keys to success is taking every experience life brings you and repackaging it in a way that empowers you and helps you to move forward.

Small Is the New Big

In big business, change used to be linear. A company could look several years down the road and plan ahead. The cost of launching a business to compete with entrenched players was beyond the reach of many would-be entrepreneurs. As a result, the lack of innovation and competition meant big companies could move at a snail's pace.

That was yesterday. Today change occurs at an exponential rate, and the pace of innovation is unparalleled. The cost for an entrepreneur to jump into a market and compete head to head with industry giants has dropped dramatically and no longer is a barrier to entry. The Internet, mobile technologies, and a virtual workforce have taken away many of the advantages once held by those with deep pockets.

This shift represents a big problem for big business: Deep-rooted cultures at most large companies make it difficult for them to keep up. Those that remain inflexible and unwilling to change the way they approach today's competitive world will die from the inside out.

This shift is good news for today's flexible entrepreneurs, who can move faster, get closer to customers, respond more quickly to changes in the marketplace, and operate their businesses for a fraction of the cost. These entrepreneurs don't resist the pace of change. They embrace it. In the new world order, small is the new big.

Here's how fast a small company can move in and disrupt an entire business.

Under the previous paradigm, a company created a product or service. It was a hit, and over time the company got bigger. It continued to add new features and started raising prices. The company could do this because the demand was there and it had little competition.

Then one day, a customer looks at his credit-card bill and says, *I don't want to pay all that money anymore.* The customer also realizes he needs only one thing, actually, the original thing he signed up for. *I don't need all this other stuff,* he says. *And I certainly don't want to pay for what I don't want.*

So the customer decides to start his own company. He plans to strip out all the fancy features he does not want to pay for and build one thing, the very same thing he currently does like in the big company's product. This aspiring entrepreneur might be eight years old or eighty; it really doesn't matter. He quickly finds a free legal service online and incorporates, sets up an account with Google to get free e-mail, contacts, calendar, office applications, and document storage. He gets free voice and video calling through Skype, free WiFi at the corner coffee bar. The entrepreneur syncs everything between laptop and mobile phone.

The business is established—in an elapsed time of, say, *ninety minutes*.

Next our entrepreneur gets down to business and goes online to do some research. A few Internet searches produce market data and access to free reports. By poking around social-media platforms like Facebook and Twitter, he can quickly find out if others think his idea has legs. Our founder logs on to LinkedIn to share the news of his new venture and seek some help. A developer who likes the idea and hates big companies volunteers to do a little coding. The new team collaborates, using free software to write a business plan.

To sum up, a customer of a big business can identify a problem and establish a company to meet that need in one afternoon. He has access to much of the same market information as the competition. Social-media conversations lead to the drafting of a business plan and the assistance of a developer who starts building the product. These people are executing—on the first day—and they've spent zero dollars so far.

This new little company builds something really basic, a minimum viable product with one feature and one benefit. What they release is pretty crude but—check this out—they give it away for free. Other people who have the same problem with the same big company's product flock to the new business. The big company is too slow to recognize what is happening and therefore too slow to respond with an alternative solution. It bleeds market share to the start-up. And a new entrepreneur is launched, with a product and a team and a market, the building blocks of a multimillion-dollar business.

Our theoretical business happens to be a technology company, but the process is the same across the board. It all started with one unhappy customer who had a laptop, a mobile phone, an Internet connection, and a social-media account. One customer who decided to take matters into his own hands and ultimately launched a better solution.

When big, entrenched industry leaders observe this happening from their spacious headquarters, it's terrifying because it's definitive proof that the scales have tipped. Even their best ideas may not work because their companies will take too long to execute.

This is an opportunity for today's entrepreneur, but it's also the reason I consult with businesses large and small all over the world, teaching them how to create a more entrepreneurial culture. Does your business culture allow for the kind of fast action required to compete in the entrepreneur economy? If not, you're in deep trouble. Today more than ever, nimble creatures adapt while the dinosaurs die off.

It reminds me of a conversation I had on Necker Island with Richard Branson while attending a conference at his Caribbean home (on his own island, in fact). I told him that my whole life had been lived in launch mode, opening new markets where we had to educate customers to their needs at the same time we were selling to them. I pointed out he had often taken the opposite approach. "You go into the biggest markets with the most entrenched customers and go head to head," I said to Richard.

As usual, Branson's response was enlightening. He said, "I go into big markets where people have already proven they want the product and will pay for it. Their wallets are already open. Then I just look for one person that has a problem. Find that one person and one problem, and if the market is big enough, that represents a big business opportunity. And that's what I do." Even though Branson's companies were making huge moves, he still thought like a smaller entrepreneur, creating new businesses to solve one problem better than the current companies in that space.

Today it's your turn to take advantage of the opportunities that entrepreneurs have today over big business, to disrupt and create innovative products and services that have a positive and lasting impact. Now that we've established some key beliefs about entrepreneurship, let's talk how we'll embark on this launch process together.

A Playbook, Not a Textbook

I hate textbooks. I don't think I've ever made it through one—too long, too boring, packed with too much information that doesn't seem relevant.

Since my goal is to give you everything you need to take your big idea to market in ninety days or less, this book is designed more like a playbook than a textbook. I've taken big concepts and broken them down into smaller, more digestible pieces.

In this book I'll share my personal experiences launching new businesses, products, and services. These experiences range from being an entrepreneur inside bootstrapped start-ups to being an executive inside some of the world's largest global brands. These stories will provide lessons that can be applied immediately, as we move quickly from the personal side of entrepreneurship into the strategies and tactics necessary to bring your vision to life.

In each chapter we will focus on one concept or action, the single most important thing you need to do in that area. With so much on your plate, asking you to do more would only slow you down rather than lead to a better result. What I know from experience is that if you commit to each lesson and follow through on each exercise, you will set yourself up for a successful launch.

Since we only have ninety days to get you to market, this book is designed to be read and implemented quickly. That means you should be able to get through each section in under five minutes.

We're going to move fast, but before we dive in, I want to make sure you have the right mind-set for making this leap. If you're reading this book, you're either interested in launching a new venture now or preparing to do so in the very near future. It doesn't matter if you are an entrepreneur or a manager of a big business who needs to think quickly on your feet in a fast-changing industry. You need the skills and lessons in this book to put you in the best position to succeed. So let's begin by eliminating a few negative beliefs that may be holding you back from launching your new project, and offer new, empowering ideas to put in their place.

Don't worry about all that talk about a slumping economy. That's nothing more than a distraction. Too many people will use it as an excuse. Despite anything you may have heard, there's no shortage of opportunity out there. The key to finding success as an entrepreneur is seizing an opportunity and, when you find it, executing like crazy.

There's never a bad time to start a business. Great fortunes have been created during good and bad times, and from some very unusual places. Sara Blakely (you'll meet her later) instinctively understood she had a big idea when, at age twenty-six, she decided to cut the feet off a pair of pantyhose. She didn't let her bank account or lack of industry experience hold her back. Today, at age forty-two, Sara retains full ownership of her undergarment company, Spanx, and last year *Forbes* magazine declared that she was a billionaire.

Value your insights. Plant this little lesson from Blakely's success in your mind: A unique insight into what the consumer wants, backed up by focus, discipline, and hard work, can and will pay off.

Age doesn't matter. You can't be too young or too old to launch a successful enterprise. Nick D'Aloisio, the British inventor who sold his mobile application, Summly, to Yahoo! for a reported thirty million dollars, did so at age seventeen, but the average entrepreneur who earns one million dollars (and does not lose it) doesn't get started with his or her successful business until age forty-one. Many don't make their first million until they're fifty or older.

Ten thousand hours? Not required. Forget the idea that you need to spend ten thousand hours doing something in order to become really successful at it. That makes great reading in Malcolm Gladwell's *Outliers,* and it might well apply to artistic skills like violin playing or painting or to athletic prowess in basketball or tennis. But it doesn't always apply to business.

Reed Hastings had virtually no video experience when he founded Netflix. Janus Friis and Niklas Zennström founded Skype despite having very little background in telecom. What did Richard Branson know about airlines or mobile phones? Nothing. Larry Ellison, Mark Zuckerberg, Mark Cuban, Jeff Bezos, Larry Page, and Sergey Brin all perfected something about which they began as less than experts—and became billionaires in the process.

Don't worry about being second in the marketplace. Entrepreneurs do not operate in a vacuum but rather in a diverse ecosystem. What one innovator creates opens up opportunities for the next generation of go-getters. The more disruption, the more opportunity. If you see a product or service out there that people already use, but you have an idea that would improve upon it in any way, you should be encouraged, not discouraged, by someone else already playing in that space and proving there is real demand for it.

Don't be afraid to try again. If you've tried to launch a business before, but things went sideways instead of up, you are not alone. Having taken a shot at entrepreneurship in the past, you'll recognize elements in this book that you missed the first time around. Maybe tough economic conditions, changes in the work-place, or unemployment put you out of position, but now you're ready to blaze your own path. Perhaps you have an existing business that you want to take to the next level. Wherever you are, upon reading these pages you'll find lots of helpful little things, distinctions you can make to identify new directions that will help you grow and scale your company.

HOW TO TURN AN INDUSTRY ON ITS HEAD

Start with One Person: In a big market, look for one customer who already has his wallet out but is unhappy about one thing in a given product or service. The odds are that, if the market is big enough, lots of people share his view. Fix that one thing.

Make Things Simple: The more complex the common practices are in your industry, the greater is the opportunity to disrupt them by simplifying them. It may not be easy, but if it were, everyone would be doing it. Solving the hard problem makes a great opportunity.

Slash Prices Dramatically: If you use technology or other systems that significantly reduce your costs relative to the competition, pass those savings on to customers. Entrenched players may not be able to compete because their infrastructure does not allow it.

(continued on next page)

(continued from previous page)

Get Close to Your Customer: Build a better relationship with your customers than anyone else in the market has. Translate that relationship into new products and services that better address their needs and desires.

. . . .

Be You: Be authentic in everything you do and transparent to the marketplace.

Find a Way to Simple

Let's tackle one more story before we get started. I credit this one to Stanley Kirk Burrell.

A few years ago I attended a conference on the Big Island of Hawaii. The organizer, David Hornik of venture-capital firm August Capital, calls the invitation-only meeting "the Lobby." Almost everything leading up to the arrival was secret; no one knew who else would be there.

On the first day the organizers issued the participants different-colored T-shirts, and we were told to go find other people wearing the same color. These people would be our team for the day. Mine consisted of Dick Costolo, now the CEO of Twitter; Sarah Lacy, the founder of PandoDaily (the leading Silicon Valley technology news site); and Bill Tai, a leading venture capitalist. But we were missing one person from our team. Looking around, we finally found our man: Stanley Burrell.

Aka MC Hammer. Rapper. Dancer. Actor.

And entrepreneur. Don't think for a second that the legendary rapper was invited to the event for entertainment value. Hammer regularly attends these industry gatherings and has invested in notable tech start-ups, including Square and Bump Technologies. He's lectured at Stanford and Harvard on the uses of social media and has a promotional deal with iPad case maker ZAGG. He's also launched businesses of his own. In 2007 the creator of hits including "U Can't Touch This" and "2 Legit 2 Quit" launched DanceJam.com, a (sadly short-lived) YouTube-like site for dancers to share videos.

Needless to say, I was psyched to be on his team.

We all climbed into a big white van. Our job was to go on a scavenger hunt, competing against other teams to be the first group to solve a series of puzzles. We were a savvy bunch, and I could sense the competitive energy surging. We got to the first site and read the clues. Our task was apparently to take a pile of rocks, a couple of sticks, and a piece of rope and turn them into something. Dick and Sarah and Bill and I looked at the materials, then looked at one another. We were confused and couldn't figure out how to solve the problem. And Hammer wasn't helping. He stood a short distance away, talking on his cell phone, looking at the ocean.

"Hey Hammer, can you help us out?" we asked.

"Yeah sure, give me the clue," he said.

Hammer took one look at the clue, thought about the problem for a minute, then proceeded to stack one item on top of another, completing the assignment. Problem solved and task completed.

We went to the next clue. The same thing happened—four of us working hard to solve the problem, Hammer talking on his phone and gazing at the ocean. When we asked him for help, he walked over, took one look at the clue, and again solved the puzzle. We moved on to the next clue. Guess what happened? He solved it again, quickly. I think Hammer solved every problem on the scavenger hunt for the team that day.

We didn't end up winning (we found out later the other groups were getting ahead of us because they were sharing clues on a new service—Twitter—cofounded by a fellow participant in the Lobby, Evan Williams). But later at the hotel, a little bit in awe, I went over to Hammer and asked him how he had managed to solve every problem so quickly. What was his secret?

"The problem with you entrepreneurs," he said, "is that you get all caught up in the details. You start off with these big goals but you make things complicated, more complicated than they need to be."

He went on. "I have a philosophy in life and business," said Hammer. "I find a way to simple first."

That was a big moment for me. When I think back on it, I associate his insight with the paper clip. The Post-it note. The Band-Aid. The toilet-paper roll. Scotch tape. The BIC pen. The disposable razor. Spanx. And a hundred—no, a thousand—other products that have one thing in common: They're incredibly simple. And they were invented only in the last 150 years. Look around your home or office. You're surrounded by simple inventions that are easy to use, that solve one problem and solve it perfectly well.

The same is true with businesses: Simple businesses are thriving everywhere. Coffee shop. Sandwich shop. Dry cleaner. Lawn service. Bar. Taxi service. It doesn't have to be complicated. Every day entrepreneurs take a tried-and-true business idea, apply some differentiation and branding, and *voilà!* Of course, there are other factors—the right location or the know-how to make awesome coffee or sandwiches—but the point is that there are thousands of business owners out there making a great living by doing simple things well.

Take Stanley Burrell's brilliant insight as an order, a compulsion, a rule for your life. It should be a rule for your whole business, truly: Your vision, operating plan, and financial model need to be so succinct and simple that you can fit them all on one page or explain it to someone in thirty seconds.

Narrow your focus. Narrow the problem. Narrow the customer. Narrow the geography. Get the whole idea as simple as you can make it, and work out from there.

Remember: Find a way to simple first.

STAGE I.

THE PRELAUNCH CHECKLIST

Thirty Days to Prepare

CHAPTER 1.

WHAT'S YOUR BIG IDEA?

Most people fail in life not because they aim too high and miss,
but because they aim too low and hit. And many don't aim at all.
—LES BROWN

How to Buy a Rainforest

I hate mosquitoes. I hate everything about them. But a few years ago
I found myself on my way to a place named . . . Moskito Island.

With night falling, the Virgin Group's global leadership team and
about forty Virgin CEOs from around the world climbed into small
boats. We were in the Caribbean for "the Gathering," as Richard
Branson called the event, to share and exchange information and
grow from one another's experiences. We shoved off from Necker
Island, which has been Richard's private retreat for about twenty
years, heading toward the nearby island he had just purchased.

Unlike Necker Island, Moskito is no resort. It's completely
deserted—there's nothing on the lump of land—and by the time
we got there, the sky was pitch-black. We were on the water about

as far east in the Caribbean as we could be. As we approached the island, no lights greeted us until we circled around to the opposite side, where tiki torches flickered on the lone strip of beach.

We went ashore and grabbed dinner at a small buffet. Looking for a place to sit and eat, I came across Richard and a group of Virgin executives eating and talking passionately about something that Richard apparently wanted to purchase.

I sat down on the beach next to him and chimed in, asking what was it he wanted to buy.

"The rainforest."

I asked which rainforest.

"The Amazon," he replied. (I guess if you're going to buy a rainforest, it might as well be the biggest one!)

I was shocked. How can you buy a rainforest? Knowing Richard, I can't say I was totally surprised he would think so big but still, my mind reeled as I thought about this proposal. I mean, who even owns the rainforest? Whom would you buy it from?

The talk continued and swirled around the positive impact you could have if you controlled the rainforest. Richard pointed out that you could stop the slashing and burning of vegetation, save precious animals that are being killed or taken out of their environment for sale, and help slow global climate change. These are issues that Richard has been passionately dedicated to for years. He's donated millions for environmental protection and has even teamed up with alternative medicine researcher Chris "Medicine Hunter" Kilham to tour the Amazon rainforest in search of indigenous pharmaceutical plants that may be cultivated someday in the jungles (by the people who are now destroying them) and sold through the Virgin Group. On Necker Island, Branson has also done his part to protect rainforest animals, creating a sanctuary for endangered Madagascar lemurs.

Someone finally interrupted this passionate conversation and said what I was thinking: "You could never buy the rainforest."

Richard got this look in his eyes that I'd never seen there before. Looking back, I remember seeing the same look in the eyes of other global leaders. It said: *How can you get in the way of possibility?* I've come to understand that a positive and resourceful outlook is absolutely essential for any entrepreneur to turn his or her big idea into a reality. And by that I mean, entrepreneurs need to understand the key difference between *having* resources and *being* resourceful.

None of the successful people I know started with everything they needed; they had to assemble what they required every step of the way. They understood—as Richard did, as does Tony Robbins—that you can back your way out of any problem that stands between you and your dream.

Look at it this way. You have an idea. No matter how big or small, the idea lives inside you, it drives you, it keeps you up late at night. Naysayers may think it impossible, but that's just because they've never seen it done before. Or maybe you believe something's possible but you're not convinced you're the one to do it. It may take capital and people and other things you just don't have. But in the world according to Branson, those are just obstacles to be overcome.

Back at the beach on Moskito Island, Branson responded to the challenge of what I thought was an impossible task, buying the rainforest, by walking us through a simple exercise.

"First of all," Branson said, "*imagine* you wanted to buy the rainforest. How would you do it?" He started peppering us with questions.

Do you have to buy the rainforest, or can you lease it? Whoa! That is a huge shift in mind-set! Let's say we could lease it. How many people do we know with significant wealth who could contribute to leasing the rainforest and, more important, get behind our cause? Better yet, think of how many people in this world would do whatever they could to contribute, even a small amount, to such a noble cause. Coming up with the money should not be a problem.

He continued to probe. Each answer inspired a deeper belief and greater confidence that it could actually be done. Within five minutes, Richard Branson made buying the rainforest sound easier than eating a bowl of soup. That's partly the difference between Richard Branson and everyone else. Most of us have yet to open ourselves up to the same sense of possibility. But *Richard*? Given enough time and the right people on the task, there's nothing that he—or, when I thought about it, any one of us—can't accomplish.

Five years later I saw that Richard was really on to something. Ecuador launched a novel initiative to protect the Yasuní Park rainforest, a place that is thought to be the single most ecologically diverse place in the world, featuring more individual species of trees in one spot than are present in all of North America, not to mention bats and birds, amphibians and reptiles. But this wasn't a simple situation where the Ecuadorians could afford to do the right thing and set the place aside for posterity. Beneath Yasuní Park are massive deposits of oil, worth billions of dollars, awaiting exploitation.

Some Branson-style creative thinking found a possible solution. In 2007, to protect Yasuní yet still bring in money for Ecuador, the government tried to effectively lease the rainforest. If donors from around the world agree to pay $3.6 billion dollars, Ecuador would promise not to allow drilling in Yasuní. Hundreds of millions of dollars were raised to compensate the government for lost revenues, thanks to monies from governments and individuals around the world, including Al Gore, Leonardo DiCaprio, and a host of environmentalists and scientists. Although the Yasuní-ITT Initiative ultimately was unable to raise enough money to meet their goals, it's clear that crowdsourcing environmental protection did catch some significant attention and could still do the future of the planet untold good.

Richard Branson's thinking that evening on Moskito Island left me deeply impressed both by the intensity of his conviction—and because he made the seemingly impossible sound easy. He took a big problem, one that seemed almost larger than life, and chunked it down into smaller, more manageable pieces. He looked to back out of a big idea, one step at a time, to reach a goal. Because he was so open to possibility, he asked better questions of the group, eliciting more productive responses and solutions.

Richard is far from alone in setting lofty goals and doing something to accomplish them. There are dozens of examples of entrepreneurs who have tried and succeeded with revolutionary ideas that at first seemed so big as to be impossible for mere mortals. They saw openings, came up with solutions, and applied them. Sometimes the solutions seemed crazy to most people, but the entrepreneurs didn't let that stop them.

Indeed, what you'll notice in looking at the history of capitalism is that while there are myriad ways to make a fortune, the real megafortunes are held by the innovators. These folks not only think outside the box but don't even recognize that there was a box to think outside of.

Many of the most successful entrepreneurs of our age achieved their success because they were the first to grasp the potential applications of new technology. Bill Gates became Bill Gates because the mothers' club at his school bought a computer with the proceeds from a rummage sale. In eighth grade young Bill started writing code when virtually no one else his age even knew what a computer was. He saw this as an opportunity: If only he could make it easier for the average person to use one of these machines, they could be very useful. MS-DOS was born.

Steve Jobs saw that people loved personal computers and avidly used Bill Gates's operating system—but he found that not only were the machines clunky, but the Microsoft software was too. So he created his own hardware and software with Apple Computer. Twenty years later he applied the same principles to his game-changing iPhone.

A hundred years ago John D. Rockefeller saw that crude oil was being discovered all over the place but realized the guys with the oil had no way of efficiently getting it to market. He built a pipeline network, and Standard Oil (the predecessor of ExxonMobil, Chevron, and several other major oil companies) was born.

If you think about it for a second, all the great dot-com fortunes were created in the same way, but instead of being inspired to move oil in a new way, these innovators figured out how to move data over fiber-optic cables. Jeff Bezos thought it would be pretty cool to be able to buy stuff over the Internet. Amazon.com was born. Mark Cuban started Broadcast.com because he wanted a way to stream college basketball games over the Internet. He sold it to Yahoo! for $5.9 billion. Mark Zuckerberg knew students at Harvard wanted a way to connect with one another over the Internet. Facebook was the result. Larry Page and Sergey Brin were frustrated by how hard it was to find what they were looking for on the Internet. Enter Google.

All these entrepreneurs had breakthroughs that began as either "crazy ideas" or improvements upon what someone else had tried. They did it first, or they did it better.

So the next time someone throws out a wacky idea—say, printing books on a press, using electricity to light a house, broadcasting radio waves, watching moving pictures on a television, surfing the Internet, developing commercial spaceflight, or buying a rainforest—know that there is someone out there who thinks with no limitations, who's assembling the right resources and is intent upon making his or her dream come true. Of course, that person might be you.

HOW TO BRING YOUR PROJECT TO LIFE

Get Clear: What is your big idea? What is keeping you up at night? What would you pursue if you knew you could not fail?

. . . .

Break Your Big Idea into Small Pieces: No matter how big the vision, you will always improve your chances of success by breaking the job down into smaller bite-size pieces and attacking them one at a time.

. . . .

Be Resourceful: Nobody starts out with everything they need to succeed. The best entrepreneurs are resourceful enough to pick up the pieces along the way.

. . . .

Surround Yourself with Great People: Find role models at every step of the way who have accomplished what you set out to achieve. Find out how they did it: Learn their beliefs, their strategies, and the order in which they did things.

. . . .

Execute Like Crazy: Outwork, outthink, and outsmart the competition.

• • •

Oil Right Under Your Feet

Between the time I spent in the training business and my breaking into technology, I got stuck in transition. In the early 1990s I worked at a bar and lived near the beach in Santa Monica. I was really struggling to find my way, wondering what direction I should take next.

I had always liked creating and building things, so I decided I wanted to build companies next. The possibility of making a fortune while making a difference was attractive, but I didn't know where to get started. How many times in your life have you been ready to make a move but couldn't seem to find the right opportunity? I kept asking myself, how was I going to make an impact? How was I going to put my ambition to work? I looked for the right place to plug in, but nothing seemed to fit.

Then a friend gave me a book that helped set me on my entrepreneurial path. Called *Losing My Virginity: How I Survived, Had Fun, and Made a Fortune Doing Business My Way,* it was the autobiography of a British guy—yes, that one—named Richard Branson.

If anybody had told me then that I would actually work with him someday, I would have been thrilled. The book inspired me in many ways and helped me think about my future from a whole new perspective. *Losing My Virginity* got me to try new ideas, to take a few chances, and to put myself into a better position to discover my Big Idea.

The first conclusion I reached then (this was twenty years ago) was that the future was *China*. I read a lot of business books, and everybody seemed to be talking about business in the Far East. I decided I would enroll in a class to learn the language and look for opportunities to work with Chinese companies. Now, I think maybe I got hooked on the idea of China because I couldn't seem to find an opportunity near me. At the time, California was in a deep economic recession and I figured I'd have to go thousands of miles away—literally to the other side of the globe—to find a place where I could make money.

Pretty smart idea, I thought, but soon I discovered the truth of that old saying that sometimes being lucky is better than being smart. In a piece of accidental timing, I was introduced to a man named Al Checchi just one week before I was scheduled to take my first Chinese class. He had worked on a business deal with my mother and she shared with him how hard I was trying to find my way. He offered to help. That meeting changed the course of my life once more.

Al had started off working for Bill Marriott, helping to build the Marriott hotel empire. In the 1980s he had moved on to work as a deal maker for the billionaire Bass brothers of Fort Worth, Texas. The Basses had made their money in oil and then diversified in all sorts of directions. One of their biggest holdings was a controlling stake in the Walt Disney Company, a deal that Checchi had personally overseen. At the time, Checchi reported to legendary moneyman Richard Rainwater, who eventually became a billionaire in his own right.

When I met Al, he was cochairman of Northwest Airlines. He asked me what was I going to do with the rest of my life. I told him my future certainly wasn't in California. Instead, I explained, my destiny was in China, because that's where all the opportunities were.

Al listened, looked hard at me, and then started talking. He told me that years earlier, just like me, he had struggled to figure out his path, imagining himself running all over the world pursuing lots of different projects. But his boss at the time had told him a simple story about a man who had been on a similar quest.

The guy spent all his life and his entire fortune searching for diamonds. Eventually he ended up in Texas. Since there's a lot of very old rock in central Texas, he felt pretty confident of a big score. The prospector hunted and hunted and dug and dug on the land he'd purchased. After weeks in the Texas sun, the back of the man's neck was tanned as dark as saddle leather, and his aching back would never be the same. But still no diamonds. Finally the man decided to give up and left town. He was so disappointed that, in a moment of anger, he sold the land for a dollar.

The buyer of his land, Al told me, was an oil wildcatter. This guy had a different hunch about what was to be found in that earth. He proved himself right when, drilling the very first well, he struck oil.

I'm not sure he needed to, but Al gave me the moral of the story. "Everything you're looking for is right here," he told me. "*It's right under your feet.*"

There is nothing like having a great mentor to point this out to you, a person who has already been down the road you are traveling, someone who is not as close to the situation and therefore has perspective. Like the diamond prospector, we can have such a fixed focus that we can't look at the bigger picture in a new way. Sometimes we're just not open-minded enough to recognize the opportunities around us, but they are there, every single day, in every direction you look, globally, locally, everywhere.

Your job is to look again. You probably don't have to go to the Great Wall, because the answer may be closer than you think. As for me . . . it turned out Silicon Valley was just up the road.

Are You Sitting on Top of a Billion-Dollar Idea?

She bought a new pair of cream-colored pants, planning to wear them to a party. But when Sara Blakely, a twenty-six-year-old Floridian, put them on and looked in the mirror, she didn't like how her butt looked. Panty lines ruined the whole effect, and she needed to find some kind of shape wear to smooth them over, fast. So she cut the feet off a pair of pantyhose, put the cream slacks back on, and headed out to the party.

Little did she realize at the time that she was about to tap into tremendous entrepreneurial opportunity. Even though her first little experiment didn't provide the perfect solution—the hose kept rolling up her legs that evening—it kicked off a process. Plus, she really, *really* wanted her invention to work. Her moment of inspiration, born out of a combination of necessity and vanity, became her Big Idea.

Sara, you see, was a born entrepreneur. As a youngster she created haunted houses and charged neighborhood kids admission. As a teenager she set up an unlicensed, unapproved babysitting business at a nearby Hilton Hotel, watching kids for eight dollars an hour. She was a cheerleader and a debate champion, but one with an especially strong desire to succeed on her own terms. She listened to tapes her dad had lying around, including Dr. Wayne Dyer's *How to Be a No-Limit Person*. She played them so many times she practically memorized them.

For a time, not everything in her life fell into place as she hoped. After trying and failing to get into law school, Sara found jobs selling office supplies, even hustling fax machines door to door. Then she learned how to cold-call and realized she was a natural salesperson, with an ego impervious to rejection. At age twenty-five, she became her company's national sales director. Her life was starting to get on track—and then those cream-colored slacks came along and changed everything.

Sara was convinced there was a way to make her idea work and she did. With five thousand dollars saved up, she invested in her vision for the future of underwear. By day she worked full time selling office supplies; at night she researched patents and studied fabrics. However, she was turned away by numerous stocking manufacturers, who weren't about to take the time to help her make a prototype.

When she finally figured out how to keep the abbreviated hose from riding up her legs, she saved money and wrote her own patent. She also found a factory willing to produce the garments; its operator was a man whose daughters thought Sara's idea so great they forced their dad to make it. Sara came up with a name for her big idea too: Spanx.

She designed her own flashy packaging and set about selling her new product. Her wares went on sale at upscale department stores like Neiman Marcus, Bloomingdale's, and Saks. When she didn't think Spanx was getting prominent enough placement at Neiman Marcus, she bought her own display rack, snuck it in, and set it up by the cash register.

Armed with all her chutzpah and desire, Blakely got a break that even she couldn't have dreamed of when, in 2000, Oprah Winfrey touted Spanx as her favorite product of the year. The orders came rolling in, and Sara finally quit her day job.

Sara cracked the code of entrepreneurship and made it work for her: She took a perceived need and, with her business instincts, made it a business. Her story has some lessons for all of us. Consider these:

Think big. From the start, Sara's vision was to sell to *millions* of women. Remember that the size of your vision will help determine the size of your success, that almost every franchise, big brand, and major product began in the mind of a single entrepreneur.

Embrace failure. From an early age, Sara put herself out there— cold-calling, selling door to door, and learning how not to take rejection or failure personally. Failing is an integral part of being an entrepreneur. Accept it, use it to your advantage, and move on.

Leverage technology. When Sara started Spanx fifteen years ago, she had to use the Yellow Pages to find someone willing to make her prototypes. Today you can research everything on the Internet. Technology can help in other ways too; the advent of 3-D printing, for example, has made it very easy to produce prototypes of many consumer goods.

Be inspired. Spanx made $4 million in its first year; today the company has sales of $250 million a year. Sara still owns 100 percent of her business and in 2012, at age forty-one, she was named by *Forbes* the youngest self-made woman billionaire in the world. To do this she didn't need to reinvent the wheel. And you, whether you're an entrepreneur or an intrapreneur (fighting inside a big organization), don't necessarily have to either. Sometimes a key improvement or iteration can change everything.

Think about the return on Sara's investment: from five thousand dollars in savings to a billion dollars. She had been looking for an opportunity, working hard to find it, and all that time she'd been sitting on her big idea.

Let Go of Your Nut!

We all have our reasons for not getting started. Unlike Sara, who was ready to jump right into entrepreneurship, some of us may be more hesitant to take the leap. As a result, we create excuses and put up roadblocks for ourselves. Do any of these sound familiar?

It's too late.
I'm too tired. I'm hungry.
I have to feed my kids.
My boss would never let me do it.
The dog needs to be walked.

I can't afford it.

The project's too big.

People will think I'm crazy.

I can't do that and do the job I have.

I don't know the right people.

I didn't go to the right school.

The company would never get behind this.

How will I get paid for it?

I'll just start tomorrow.

And the biggest one of all?

I'm afraid.

Unfortunately, our fears, combined with the crazy stories we tell ourselves about why we can't succeed, keep us from getting started.

In order to bring your big idea to life, the first step I want you to take is to let go of all your excuses. Simply step away and get on with it.

Let me put it another way: *Don't be a spider monkey.*

The spider monkey may be the most elusive animal in the rainforest. It's so quick, you can't sneak up on one of these wily little forest creatures with a net. It's way too fast for that. But bestselling author and speaker Greg Reid tells a useful story about how to successfully trap the spider monkey by playing to its weakness.

The spider monkey possesses the human tendency to grab on to things that he thinks he can't live without. Then he refuses to let go.

Greg describes the strategy of the successful spider-monkey hunter. All he needs to do is find a log in the rainforest, drill a hole about eighteen inches deep, and drop a couple of peanuts down the hole.

That's it. In time, a spider monkey will happen along and smell the delicious peanuts. He'll reach his arm down the hole and grab them. But the hole is sized such that, when the monkey closes his hand around the peanuts, the monkey's clenched fist gets stuck in the hole. He could open his hand, drop the peanuts, and pull his hand out of the hole. But he can't do both. He can't get the peanuts and get free.

Long ago, native hunters discovered that they could drop the bait in the hole, then just wander off for an hour or two. When they came back, all they had to do was drop a net over the stubborn monkey. The monkey was so obsessed with those peanuts that he just kept his hand in there, holding on tight, even as the hunter closed in.

My advice to you: *Let go of that nut!* Don't be that monkey. Let go of those fears, excuses, and stories you have made up about why you can't succeed. Let go of those things that hold you back.

Maybe you're holding on to a fear of failure or a regret from the past. Maybe it's a fear of the unknown. Maybe it's a dead-end job you can't bring yourself to walk away from, a bad relationship, destructive habits, or the wrong kind of friends. Got anything you want to add to the list?

Like that monkey, we believe what we're holding on to is more important than anything else, maybe even that it's going to save us. Ultimately, this thinking will just lead to failure and frustration.

So quit holding yourself back. Stop focusing on reasons and start focusing on results. Beethoven went deaf, but among his late-in-life works is some of the greatest music man has ever heard. Milton was blind, but he wrote literature that will be read until the end of time. Whatever your excuse is, it isn't good enough. The only thing that's keeping you from having everything you want is the story you keep telling yourself about why you can't have it.

So drop the peanut. Just let it go. Then try climbing a tree to see what opportunities lie on the other side.

LETTING GO

What would happen if you decided to let go? How would your life change if you really decided to go for it? What would happen if you made your biggest dreams come true?

Would you spend more time with your family? Would you pick up a hobby? Would you buy a new home? Would you travel around the world and check items off your bucket list? Would you create a charitable organization that gave back to others?

The only thing keeping you from achieving everything you want in your life is the crazy story you've made up about why you can't have it. Now is the time to seize your opportunity and create the life you deserve.

CHAPTER 2.

PROTECTING WHAT'S MOST IMPORTANT

My mama always used to tell me: "If you can't find somethin' to
live for, you best find somethin' to die for."

—TUPAC SHAKUR

The Sure Thing

Have you ever had a "sure thing"? An idea for a business or product that was just so good, you knew it could not fail? When you
shared the idea with others, their jaws dropped. As you got
started, everything fell into place: Your timing, your team, and
your execution were flawless. You *knew* you could not lose. So
you doubled down; maybe you put everything you had on the line.

I've been there as well. In 2005 I was closing in on a deal to run
a new Internet business when I got a call from my good friend Jason
Port. He had heard I was in the market for a new business opportunity and encouraged me to take a look at private aviation.

After 9/11, he told me, private aviation's growth had skyrock-
eted. Passengers on commercial flights had grown frustrated with

increased travel times, long lines at security, having to remove their shoes, and the rest of it. Private-jet charter had suddenly emerged as a terrific option for business travelers. He also told me that, despite its growth, private aviation remained highly inefficient, so there might be a good opportunity for skilled Internet entrepreneurs to help the industry operate more efficiently.

I looked at the charter business. The numbers showed growth in users and revenue like I hadn't seen since the dot-com boom, but the business was highly fragmented. In commercial aviation there were a handful of operators, like American, Continental, United, Delta, and Southwest, that controlled virtually all the passenger seats and owned hundreds of aircraft. Private aviation was completely different; there were approximately 2,500 operators in the United States alone, typically controlling only three planes each.

When it came to selling seats for commercial flights, companies like Expedia, Travelocity, and Orbitz could easily connect travelers to commercial flight schedules, making it simple to search, find, and purchase a trip online. In contrast, just as my friend had told me, the private-aviation industry was incredibly inefficient. Nobody had effectively aggregated the supply and demand in one place to make it easy to purchase a trip on a private jet. To book one you would have to find a local operator through word of mouth, by looking them up in the phone book, or by calling the local airport. Once you got a charter operator on the phone, he would then have to create a custom quote for your trip, oftentimes initiating a back-and-forth of faxes. The process was made tougher still because the guy answering the phone was sometimes the guy flying the plane!

As a result of my research, I decided to enter the market and tackle this problem. I started Smart Charter in 2006 as an online marketplace and booking tool for private aviation. Think of it as Expedia for private jets. My goal was to match up supply and demand, making the process of buying and selling trips on private jets simple.

I opened an office in Los Angeles and hired a great team (from companies like Google, Expedia, Yahoo!, Travelocity, and the Jet Propulsion Laboratory). To build the business, in September 2006 we went out to raise money, and in that process I was introduced to Richard Branson's Virgin Group. Richard was my longtime hero as an entrepreneur, and his company, Virgin, was among the most respected aviation brands in the world. In April 2007 Virgin bought a controlling interest in my company. We were rebranded as Virgin Charter. My new job was to run the business.

All of this reinforced my belief that I had a sure thing. We were in a growing market solving a big problem. Our timing, our team, and our execution had been great. Now, with Virgin as an investor, how could I lose?

So I doubled down. Went all in. I was in the right place at the right time . . . or so I thought.

We launched as Virgin Charter in March 2008. The first quarter of 2008 was incredible for private aviation. There were more private-aircraft sales, more fractional sales, and more charter hours flown than at just about any time in history. The day we launched, Richard and I went on CNBC to make the announcement. But two other news stories caught my attention that day: concerns about an economic recession and a spike in oil prices. That's when I feared things might begin to change, and not for the better.

The business started to go sideways, quickly. In the first half of 2008 oil prices went soaring. Typically, airlines pass along fuel costs to their customers, but in 2008 prices were rising so fast that there was no time for them to recoup their costs fast enough. Rapidly rising oil prices destroyed the business model for many airlines almost overnight. While that was bad news for the big commercial airlines, they had an advantage we did not have in private aviation: many more passengers to share increased fuel costs. For charter operators, it wasn't that simple. It was not uncommon for only one person to be on board the private aircraft, so the cost for that passenger's flight was much higher. At launch in March 2008, the average charter of a private jet from Los Angeles to New York sold for approximately $30,000. A few months later, fuel costs had pushed that up to almost $45,000. Let me tell you, that kind of massive price hike is a disaster.

Predictably, a chain reaction followed. People who would previously charter big planes instead went with small ones. People who used to take long trips chartered planes for short ones. Many stopped chartering altogether.

Our business was burning more capital than we had planned, meaning we needed cash to survive. We decided to go and raise money to provide operating capital for the business. I was on the road for weeks and managed to secure partner meetings with three prominent venture-capital firms. But my highest hopes rested with a meeting that took place on Sand Hill Road in Silicon Valley in September 2008.

The day before the meeting, I flew from Los Angeles to the Bay Area with Brian Pope, our chief operating officer. We locked ourselves in a hotel room and prepared to give a great presentation. Upon arriving at Menlo Ventures, we were greeted by Mark Siegel, Menlo Venture's managing director and the partner leading our deal. We were taken to an office and were asked to wait until we were called into the meeting. We were so focused on preparing our pitch that neither one of us looked at the news or read the headlines that day.

When we were finally asked to join the group, there were almost fifty people in the room. They were all in the prayer position, meaning that they had their heads downs, with their thumbs furiously working the keyboards on their BlackBerry phones. There was a steady flow of assistants bringing yellow sticky notes about phone calls that needed to be returned immediately.

Everything seemed strange and tense, so I asked what was going on. One of the partners looked at me and told me that Lehman Brothers had just declared bankruptcy and the market was down five hundred points!

You won't be shocked to learn the meeting didn't go well. Everything about the world was about to change. You remember those days, when the stock market would fall three hundred points in a day, then three hundred more the next day. We were falling into the deepest recession since the Great Depression.

We didn't get the cash we needed at that time and my so-called sure thing stopped being about building something great and became all about saving what we could.

We'd started with a great idea, with timing that seemed perfect, a great team, and a solid plan. We'd gotten the Virgin Group behind us and received Richard Branson's stamp of approval. I'd gone all in, putting all my chips on the table. Sure, there were many things I could have done better. But the point is, I lost the hand.

Here's the problem with sure things: There is nothing really *sure* about them. There can't be because there are just too many moving parts in any business. Too many things that need to go right. All of which translates to an essential message: The most important job for any entrepreneur preparing to launch is to learn how to *mitigate their risk*. It's learning how to take the time up front to protect their downside. That way, if things do go sideways, they don't lose what's really important and can bounce right back.

In this chapter we'll talk about how you can protect the personal downside risk in your new venture. But let me tell you what "personal" means to me. In my office I have two napkins framed on the wall (entrepreneurs, you'll find, do a lot of their best work on the back of napkins). One is the original drawing I created of the Smart Charter Web site (the idea took shape in a coffee shop).

The other is a napkin with my wife's phone number and a little heart with the words "call me." She gave that to me when we first met. Today the business that I thought was my sure thing is gone. But what is really important, my relationship with my wife and family, is stronger than ever. Those two napkins are a daily reminder not to lose sight of what truly matters.

One truth of entrepreneurship is that everyone has ups and downs, highs and lows, and wins and losses. What's most important in each new venture is to protect yourself up front, be perfectly clear about the amount of risk you are willing to take, and learn how to mitigate that risk every step of the way. That way, if your sure thing does not work out, you don't lose what's most important and you can bounce right back.

The Fastest Way to Lose Your First Million

Ask yourself this: How much are you willing to risk? How much time and money are you willing to put on the line to make your dream come true?

Many entrepreneurs fail to get started because they are afraid of what could happen to them financially if things don't work out. They have heard stories about people who risked everything, all the money and assets they had, and then lost it all. Managers in big companies have heard similar stories about peers taking risks and their projects going upside down. Those typically end with people losing their jobs.

What they don't know is that there are several ways to limit their financial downside. Risk should *not be risky*. It should be planned and well thought out. It should be measured in advance. Systems should be put in place to ensure that even if something does not go as planned, you, your family, and even your job are protected.

Based on years of experience coaching entrepreneurs, I know that the number one mistake most make is mismanaging their money through a launch. When modeling their business, they are too optimistic. They overestimate their revenues and underestimate their expenses. Over time their business demands more cash than anticipated, so they start pulling out more and more of their own money to meet the company's needs. They get caught up in the momentum of the process, trying to balance the new demands of their business against all their other personal responsibilities. Eventually, they lose track of how much cash they really have on hand and how much has been committed to go out the door.

The result? One day they get a shocking bank statement in the mail: The money is gone, and the account has nothing left in it. The start-up capital is spent. Worse still, so is the money to pay next month's mortgage.

When the horrified entrepreneur looks back, wondering how this all came to pass, part of the explanation is obvious. You'd be amazed how many entrepreneurs launching new ventures don't go to the trouble to separate business from personal accounts. The result can lead to a significant amount of stress for any new business owner, or even personal catastrophe.

This doesn't have to happen to you. Here are the most important steps that you can apply today to make sure your financial planning is sound.

Balance your optimism. We'll talk more about this later (see "Business Planning," page 81), but the first step to mitigating your personal financial risk is to create a realistic financial model for your business. That means coming up with revenue and expense assumptions that balance your natural optimism and help determine how much cash the business will really need. Here's how you do it.

First create a list that includes all of your company's income sources and add up how much money you project your business will take in each month over the next year. Be sure not to project revenue coming in too early.

Next create a list of all your expenses. This includes all the capital it takes to start up the business, including legal fees, the cost of setting up your Web site, and payment to the various people you will need to get things off the ground. Once you have estimated these one-time start-up costs, be sure to add your monthly operating expenses to the tally: office rent, telephone bill, insurance, etc.

Finally, take your income and subtract your expenses to determine how much money you will need to start and maintain the business until it is able to pay for itself.

Once you are confident and firmly believe you have the right model in place, take your revenue projections and cut them in half. And cut them in half again. Then do it one more time for good measure. Now take your expenses and double them.

These more conservative numbers may be hard to digest, but experience suggests this approach will give you a reasonable sense of what will really occur in your business and how much time it will take before you no longer have to dip in to your own capital to make ends meet.

Determine how much money you are willing to risk. Now that you have a reference point, determine your risk tolerance: How much money can you afford to lose?

Your launch has to be funded somehow, and the odds are that much of the funding will come directly from you or, if you can get a bank or personal loan to start your business, that your name will appear on the documents as the guarantor. Unless you have a track record in business or friends with deep pockets, raising money from investors to get started may be difficult. Will the money on the line be your family's entire nest egg, or just half? Are you going to bootstrap, or borrow?

Talk everything through with your spouse or significant other. You *must* do this before jumping in with two feet. It's essential that the two of you be in agreement regarding how much to put on the line. If you don't agree, that will create problems down the road, possibly very large ones that will distract you from your business—and potentially ruin the relationship. I'd suggest you would do better to risk less and be on the same page than to risk more and have your spouse worried and resentful day after day.

Put your risk capital into a separate checking account. Do it now. Once you have a sense of the capital needed for the launch, transfer the funds you are willing to risk into a separate business checking account immediately. If your risk capital is tied up in securities or other investments, sell them and put the proceeds into the business account.

This is your seed money. Once you see it moved from your savings account to an account tied to risk, it becomes real. It focuses your attention. You see what's at stake. You have a clear financial framework to help you make better decisions, and you will act more strategically, less impulsively.

What if that business account gets low or runs out? You have a few options: You can increase your risk threshold and put more money in, find an investor or partner, or sell or close the business.

In these early stages, however, what's most important is that, by separating your business finances, you will have created a mechanism whereby you will be forced to confront decision points. You will be faced with the facts sooner rather than later. You won't accidentally run through your personal finances and allow your spending to go beyond a point that is too much for you to risk.

Keep your credit cards separate. Have one credit or debit card for business expenses, another for personal use. You need to do this as a way of tracking, accounting, and leveraging all that you can for tax purposes. Any and all expenses related to your business should be funded from this account. Don't commingle anything.

Hire a bookkeeper your first day in business. Too often, entrepreneurs wait to do this or put it off altogether, but you need someone to track revenue, expenses, assets, and liabilities. Having correct data on hand is important for you, your investors, and tax preparers. If you don't set up a system early, you will spend a tremendous amount of time and energy going back trying to reconstruct the details behind every transaction that affects your business.

The price of paying a pro will be well worth the investment. Setup may take an hour, followed by monthly, weekly, or daily updates, depending on how much activity there is in your accounts. My bookkeeper logs in to my computer each day for a few minutes and updates the day's transactions. That means I have a report every morning telling me exactly how all of my business and personal accounts are performing. Because we were set up correctly from the start, this works out to a monthly cost of $150.

Having a professional on board will have a range of other benefits. Paying attention to your books at this early stage will establish good habits at your company and instill a sense of financial responsibility throughout the organization. That sense of financial responsibility may also spill over into your personal accounts.

Have an attorney set your business up by the book. We live in a very litigious society, so you need to protect yourself from liability. Set aside money to create a proper legal entity and get business insurance. Remember, your concern isn't only about the short term; there are larger, long-term issues that you need to consider. Keep in mind too that even if this is your venture, it's not just about you.

Learn how to manage and grow your personal take. It is important to constantly expand your understanding of how money works, so that as your business grows and spills off cash, you are able to invest those profits in a meaningful way to grow your personal fortune.

If your goal is to one day create a personal financial windfall through an IPO, sale, or merger, it is important to be prepared for this possibility. Most entrepreneurs are so busy working on their business, trying to make that first million, that there is no plan in place for when they finally do. As a result, they mismanage the money and lose all or part of it. Being unprepared for success is the fastest way to lose your first million. So it's important to build a great team of advisers around you that includes bankers, brokers, accountants, and financial planners. This way, when payday finally comes, you will be ready for it.

Instead of trying to decide by yourself who should be on your team, find mentors who have made and grown their own personal fortunes. Ask them for help, guidance, and personal referrals. Their advice could be worth millions, literally.

Decide to launch one business or product at a time. Many entrepreneurs, in order to hedge their bets, try to get three or four plates spinning at once. Don't. We will talk later about the importance of focusing on one thing—I promise you, the best route to success is not to spread your energy and focus on ten things hoping one will work. Give the one thing everything you've got.

All for One and One for All

I'm a huge fan of Starbucks. Like a lot of entrepreneurs, not only am I addicted to its product, but from time to time Starbucks has served as my office. A couple years ago I had the opportunity to meet the brilliant entrepreneur and chief executive behind Starbucks, Howard Schultz, when he spoke to an entrepreneurs' group in Southern California.

Schultz had been touring in support of his book, *Onward: How Starbucks Fought for Its Life Without Losing Its Soul*. He gave a prepared talk, describing how in the late 2000s he steered Starbucks out of its crisis of overexpansion and loss of identity. He talked about reclaiming his CEO role, closing hundreds of stores and revamping hundreds of others, and how one day he shut down all 7,100 U.S. locations for three hours so baristas could get a refresher course on how to make the perfect espresso. Instead of being hell-bent on growth, Starbucks went back to being a nice place to go relax and get a good cup of joe.

It was a great story, but it sounded like a press release—it lacked candor. I wanted to hear his advice on how to be a better entrepreneur, and I know I wasn't the only one.

After the talk Schultz did a Q&A session. The last question finally proved to be the right one to open Schultz up and get him to tell us a more personal story. A man said, more or less, "I admire you, Mr. Schultz; you have an amazing story and a great product. But when you just spoke about how you were hurting when Starbucks fell on tough times, I just couldn't relate. After all, you have a billion dollars in the bank while many of the rest of us are just trying to feed our families. So please share some ways in which we all can relate to you."

The room was silent.

At that moment Howard Schultz's demeanor changed. The billionaire CEO became the Schultz of thirty years ago, a bootstrapping entrepreneur like the rest of us. The story he told will stay with me for the rest of my life and his honesty made me an even bigger fan.

In 1981 Schultz was just another Brooklyn kid looking for a break, working for Hammarplast, a Swedish coffee-machine maker. When he first arrived in Seattle, he made a sales call on Starbucks at its first—and in those days only—location at Pike

Place Market. In Schultz's recollection, the day was magical, the sky blue, the city looking as dazzling as Oz. He decided then and there he wanted to work for Starbucks.

He eventually persuaded the founders to take him on as a marketing guy but, after the owners declined to launch his idea of including an espresso bar in Starbucks, he traveled to Europe. There he acquired the rights to a coffee brand called Il Giornale. He returned to Seattle, looking to raise money to open his first Il Giornale store. He was working for no pay. His wife was pregnant with their first child.

His father-in-law flew into town from Ohio and asked Schultz to go out for a walk. They sat down on a park bench and he said to Schultz, "My daughter is seven months pregnant and her husband doesn't have a job, just a hobby. I want to ask you in a heartfelt way, with real respect, to get a job." Schultz started to cry. He was flushed with embarrassment.

He went home to his wife and, later that night, told her about the conversation. He had thought over what his father-in-law had advised, and figured he probably should sell his interest in Il Giornale and get a real job. Wisely, he asked his wife what she thought he should do.

Sheri set him straight. She gave him her *Rocky* speech (remember the one Adrian gives Rocky when he has doubts before the big fight with Apollo Creed?). Sheri told Howard that they were in this thing together, that she believed in him, that she was sure he would be able to raise the money for the coffee shop. And that he should not quit—he should go for it.

That was all he needed to hear. It was an enormous, almost irresponsible risk that Schultz took. But it paid off. He got the financing, and a few years later he acquired Starbucks.

In an ideal world, all entrepreneurs would have people like Sheri to support them in their new ventures. But that's a lot to ask.

Being a spouse, family member, or best friend of an entrepreneur is not easy. These are people who go through the wins and losses right alongside us. Sometimes they are as much at risk financially as we are. Too often we take these people for granted.

I've learned that successful ventures start at home. The first and most important job of any entrepreneur is to get on the same page as his or her spouse or significant other. If you're not in alignment, there are only two possible outcomes when things get tough: The business will suffer, or the relationship will suffer.

How do you reach a meeting of the minds? You begin by talking through a few essential questions. The most important include:

How much financial risk are you (the spouse) willing to take? If you are launching a new business, the odds are you are bootstrapping, that is, using your own money. You and your spouse need to agree upon how much you're willing to put aside and put at risk in pursuit of your dream. You need to start on the same page.

How much time will you allow me to commit? To successfully launch in ninety days, you will have to commit to your business first, with your family, along with everything else, coming second. You will have too much on the line. There will be too many moving parts for you to tend to anything other than your business, which needs to be your top priority. That doesn't mean your family is less important, just that, for a period of time, both of you agree that this is something in which you need to immerse yourself in the interests of your shared future.

How much do you want to be involved in the business? Being an entrepreneur can be a lonely job. At times it's difficult to find others to talk to about the challenges you face at the office. For example, there are certain things you may not want to share with your investors. There are certain issues that need to be kept away from employees. You usually don't want to spend your time with friends talking about problems at work. So you go home and vent.

CVO is the acronym for what I call the "chief venting officer." It is the role typically occupied by your spouse, your significant other, or a member of your family. It can be a lousy job because CVOs tend to hear about the tough stuff but not the good things that occur every day.

Like Sheri, this person is on the entrepreneurial roller-coaster ride with you. He or she is expected to support you and hold your hand through it all. Success is never easy and rarely happens overnight. When you're in a relationship, it is never a one-person effort.

There are some CVOs who really want to be involved. They want to know everything and thrive on a blow-by-blow account of the day. Others can take the ups and downs only in smaller chunks and want to hear far less. You need to be sensitive to how much your friends and family members can take.

One of the best pieces of advice I can give is to calibrate your communication strategy to suit your life partner. Do you talk about business once a day or once a week? If things are tough, do you come home and share everything before bed or wait until the end of the week to get it all out? Come to an understanding that works for both of you and respect it. How you handle the pressures of your business can either kill or strengthen your relationship.

Keep in mind that some people come from traditional business families where stability is the rule, with nine-to-five employment and a weekly paycheck for life. For people brought up in such circumstances, the seesaw of launching and entrepreneurship may be hard to handle. I am lucky that my wife, Rachel, grew up in a family of entrepreneurs. She lived through good and bad times but also saw how everyone got through them. As a result, she doesn't get rattled but even so, she doesn't want a daily blow-by-blow account of what happened in my businesses.

Rachel also taught me another essential lesson: The way you spell love in a relationship with an entrepreneur is *T-I-M-E*. That's why we make it a point to get child care every Saturday and carve out time to have lunch together. I am usually relaxed because I'm out of the office. Things that seemed urgent during the week don't matter. I get a chance to tell her what's going on and get her feedback. Having this exchange doesn't take much time, but we need to do it and do it consistently. Both sides have to be present and accounted for.

You should put in place something similar once you've found a mutually workable strategy. No matter how understanding your life partner is, you still have to prepare him or her for the challenges you'll face in building your business. Most important, you need to be in alignment with regard to how much both sides are willing to risk, how much time both sides are willing to commit, and what communication strategy works best for both of you.

TALK IT OVER

Your new venture will take significant time and resources to launch and could involve financial risk. While you are out pursuing your dream, your actions will affect the people around you. Before jumping in, make sure that you and your spouse or significant other are on the same page.

. . . .

How much time will you need to put into this new project? During launch, your business will need to be your first priority. This doesn't mean you love your family and friends any less. It does mean that during this period your business will need to come first.

How much financial risk are you willing to take? Would you rather take less financial risk and be on the same page as your spouse or take on more risk and create a problem at home?

Super Balls and Glass Balls

The entrepreneur must master the art of juggling. Your job, your finances, your spouse, your family, and maybe your boss; your health, projects, and deadlines—they're all in the air and you're always at risk of dropping one.

Some people juggle better than others and can manage to keep all those balls in the air indefinitely. Most of us, though, reach a point at which it just becomes too much and one or two will crash to the ground. We might even drop everything.

All of which makes it essential that you understand this little rule of nature: *Super Balls bounce and glass balls shatter.* You need to think about which balls are which in your life.

If you drop the Super Balls made of rubber, they will keep bouncing on their own for a while, none the worse for wear. While you're working on launching your venture, you don't have to worry so much about the ones you know to be bouncy and resilient. Later, when you can turn your attention back to them and recommit to those areas of your life, those rubber balls will take to the air again. No great harm done.

Glass balls? They're a different matter.

In the fall of 2008 the sky was falling. I was standing at the airport with Steve Ridgway, the CEO of Virgin Atlantic Airways, waiting for a plane on Tortola Island. Our businesses both faced big challenges, buffeted as we were by the harsh winds of the growing global economic crisis, which threatened the economic stability of almost every nation and institution.

My business was vulnerable. I felt vulnerable too, as if I just might blow off the Jetway at any moment, but Steve looked calm.

I asked him, "Steve, with all the pressure on you, especially right now, what's the most important part of your job?" I expected to hear something like leadership, team building, or vision.

His answer was simple, just one word.

"Exercise."

Exercise? I was surprised.

Later that day I sat next to David Cush, the CEO of Virgin America, on the flight home. I asked him the same question: "What's the most important part of your job?"

His answer? "Exercise."

Again I was shocked. David hadn't been with us when Steve and I had spoken earlier. They hadn't had a chance to compare notes, but they had both given me the same answer. Two powerful guys, running big businesses at a superdifficult time, and they both said the most important thing was *exercise*. It took awhile for this lesson to sink in, but you know what? They're right.

Launching your business will be stressful and arduous. You'll always feel like there isn't enough time for the ten thousand things you have to do, and that if you could just squeeze a couple more hours of work into the day, you'd really feel like you had something to show for it. But you can't keep going at a hundred miles per hour if you're out of gas.

We keep going by fueling our tanks. We can either choose good fuels like healthy foods and exercise or opt for a bad diet made up of things like alcohol and high-caffeine drinks, along with little to no exercise. But you know as well as I do that your physical health directly impacts your ability to perform at a high level and even influences your mental health. Exercise enables you to blow off steam and release stress, which ultimately helps to keep you calm and thinking more clearly. It's an essential component of dealing with the challenges of entrepreneurship.

Your health is a glass ball. If you drop it hard enough, it won't just break. It will shatter, and you can't be sure that you'll be able to put yourself back together again.

You may think you can't find the time, but you simply have to get out and exercise, get your body in motion every day. This doesn't mean you need to run a marathon or train as a triathlete. Thirty minutes a day will do it, even just a walk around the neighborhood. What you need more than anything is movement to get your heart pumping. You need some measurable physical activity to release the stress that comes along with your position and to recharge your body. Remember, if you don't have a way to release all the pressure, to let off steam, the stress will catch up with you. You won't have the energy or strength or endurance to do your job right. You and your business will be set up to fail.

If you have to build your day around exercise, do it. I asked Mark Moses, an überentrepreneur and triathlete you'll meet in another chapter, how somebody with a business schedule like his could fit the many hours of training it takes to be an Ironman triathlete into his day. He said, "I put my exercise into my calendar first and then schedule everything else around it. By getting in that time and training I have more energy and a clearer head than all those people who spend their entire day letting stress build up behind a desk."

You'll be surprised at how getting your mind off your work will actually help you find solutions to the toughest problems your business faces. You know how sometimes you'll have an epiphany while standing in the shower? The same thing happens to me when I'm out for a walk. When you force yourself to exercise, you may feel guilty at first because you're taking a break from work—*there's that deadline approaching!*—but in reality you're freeing up some bandwidth of your attention span. That will give your subconscious the extra processing power it needs to make breakthroughs.

So get some exercise every day. Pick a time of day that works best for you; work your schedule around it. Try to get your workout away from home; there are too many distractions there and it can be difficult to really let go. If you can, do it alone so you can let your mind wander and permit the stress to ease out of you. As an entrepreneur you have to be flexible, ready for anything. Your business may or may not be around in ten years, but you want to be.

Distinguishing the glass balls from the rubber ones isn't hard—and it's all important that you devise strategies to balance the pressures so you don't shatter what is most important in your life. When times get tough, you need to be the toughest person in the room. You can't be ready if you don't take care of yourself.

Ten Thousand Reasons Why You Will Succeed

One of the biggest challenges entrepreneurs face is the emotional roller coaster they ride every day when launching a business.

You wake up in the morning, an investment comes through, and then you lose it. Suddenly the money is back. The product is working as planned, then it goes down, and now it's back up. The key employee you want to hire is a go but unexpectedly falls out. Later he agrees to sign.

Taking a seat on this roller coaster can wreak havoc on your business. The highs and lows can be exhausting. They can quickly drive you in and out of emotional states that won't help you run your business effectively, will strain your relationships, and can have a negative impact on your health.

As an entrepreneur you need to learn how to smooth out the ride and manage your emotions in a way that balances your energy, drives your business forward, and puts you in the best position to succeed, no matter what life throws at you. You can do this by *controlling your focus*. The brain works a lot like Google. It gives you answers, but those answers are only as good as the questions you ask.

When an investment falls through, the product goes down, or a new hire falls out, you begin an internal dialogue. You start asking questions to help understand what just happened and what it all means.

Most people don't understand that this dialogue is even taking place. They are conditioned to respond to circumstances in a very specific way and don't even know it. If that conditioning leads them to ask good, empowering questions, the business will go down one path. If it leads them to ask an endless loop of negative questions, their lives will go in a whole other direction.

For example, when you hit a bump in the road, if your automatic response is to start asking questions like *Why does bad stuff always happen to me?* and *Why do bad things always happen to my business?* then your Google-like brain will do a search and pull up ten thousand reasons why your business stinks. Your focus will go right to these answers, which will make you feel terrible. It's impossible to act in a way that is effective from that place.

Instead you must teach yourself to ask a better set of questions, ones that empower you and your business. Because having the right mind-set immediately shifts your focus from each challenge to the opportunity it presents.

When things weren't going your way, what would happen if you started asking questions like *What is great about this experience? What can I learn from this experience?* or *How can I use this experience to help my business succeed?* Again, your brain will run a search. But this time, you'll get ten thousand reasons why you will succeed. That is exactly what you will focus on, putting you in a much better position to drive your business forward.

If you take only one thing away from this book, this should be it: *Ask a better question*—and watch how your life changes forever.

If you want to develop a razorlike mind-set, one that cuts through problems like a knife, here's how:

Recognize that you are in complete control. Nothing in life has any meaning other than the meaning you give it. You have a choice in determining how you evaluate any situation and where you place your focus.

Break your pattern. The odds are that you have been running on autopilot most of your life, allowing your emotional state to dictate your inner dialogue. Next time you run into a problem or something threatens to knock you off course, *stop*! Pay attention to the questions you are asking to evaluate the situation, and if they are negative, interrupt your pattern with a new set of empowering questions. This will help you look at the situation in a whole new light. With enough practice, this powerful way of thinking will become automatic.

Develop new habits. Developing the skill of focusing on what empowers you is like building a muscle. Your job is to exercise your mind each and every day. The best time to start is in the morning. Take control of your focus as soon as you wake up. Begin the day by asking questions that set you up for empowerment, like *What am I grateful for? Why will I succeed? How can I move this business forward today—and have an awesome time in the process?* Starting the day with this mind-set will put you in a much better position to execute.

Never make a big decision at your lowest point. Many times it seems like we make our biggest decisions when we are in the worst possible position to think clearly. Next time, *wait*! Hold off until you ask a better question. Wait until you have physically moved to get the blood flowing, stepped away from whatever the situation is, and released some tension. You will find that you will make a much better decision from a more balanced emotional state.

Pass this skill on to your team. Imagine if everyone on your team operated from this place of razor-sharp focus, if they looked at everything that came their way as empowering tools that they could use to drive the business forward. Imagine if they were conditioned to find the opportunity to improve in every situation. Wouldn't they also be making smarter decisions?

The decision is up to you. Are you ready to take control of your life? Are you ready to get off the roller coaster?

If the answer is yes, then just do one thing—ask a better question—and focus squarely on the opportunity in everything that life presents.

Every entrepreneur needs to protect what is most important. That means you! The way to start is by mitigating your risk. This begins with keeping an eye on your finances and relationships and developing a razorlike mind-set that helps you convert any problem into an opportunity that moves your business forward. Remember, you are in much more control of the results in your life than you realize.

• • •

THE OTHER HALF OF LIFE

Controlling your focus is only one half of determining how you will behave. Another way to control how you behave is to change the way you move.

If I asked you to describe a person who was down or had had a hard day, it would be easy: eyes cast down, shoulders slumped, and breath low and shallow. If I took that same person and simply had him change the way he was using his body, had him lift his gaze, bring his shoulders back, and breathe deeply, I could take him right out of that emotional state. That is because the different ways you use your body send different signals to your brain.

Try it for yourself. The fastest way to change the way you feel is to change the way you move. As Tony Robbins would say, "Motion creates emotion." So if you are down or you are having a tough day—go out and move. Get the blood flowing. When you feel stuck in your business, no problem. Get out of your chair and take a walk outside. Movement will instantly change the way you feel and put you in a better position to take on the day.

CHAPTER 3.

YOUR ENVIRONMENT

I don't know the key to success, but the key to failure is trying to please everybody.

—BILL COSBY

Crabs in a Bucket

Nothing is more important than the people you surround yourself with. You don't need me to tell you that the right friends and contacts can help in a thousand ways, but let's examine your personal ecosystem. Odd as it may sound, I'd like you to start by thinking in terms of crabs.

Imagine you've got a bucketful of freshly caught live crabs. If you look down into the bucket, you see the crabs squirming around, as some instinct tells them it's their job to try to figure out how to escape. Individually, they're each taking a turn clawing and climbing over the others trying to get a grip on the lip of the bucket.

Should you put a lid on the bucket to prevent dinner from crawling away?

Don't worry about it. There's a funny thing about crabs—as soon as one crab looks like he's about to hoist himself up over the edge of the bucket, the other crabs grab onto him and pull him back down. They can't understand that if everyone just worked together and formed a crab chain, all the crabs on the bottom could easily climb up to the top and out of the bucket and go about their business. But no; whenever one crab starts to show some leadership, some initiative, it gets pulled all the way back down to the bottom. Eventually they just stop trying.

Have you ever felt like a crab in a bucket? Maybe your office mates criticize you for trying too hard and making them look bad. Your boss may not want you to move ahead because then he'd have to find someone else to do your busywork. Perhaps your friends think you're getting too big for your britches because you want something better for yourself than what you grew up with.

Is your entire family trapped in this mind-set? Parents often don't want their grown children to move away because they think they need them nearby to take care of them when they get older. Some spouses resent their entrepreneurial partners because, if one person is off pursuing a dream, the other person feels abandoned to raise the kids alone or do all the chores.

Life is way too short to hang around others who want to pull you down. The number one determinant of who you are and, eventually, of the results you achieve in life and business is your *environment*. Think about your environment at work, at home, in your neighborhood, in all the places you spend time. Do these places pull you down or elevate you? Do you feel good and comfortable where you work? Do your friends look out for you, encourage you, and help you brainstorm? Or do they reinforce bad habits? Do they share your values? If you have to compromise yourself and what you believe for the people around you, it's time to change the people around you.

Are the people around you invested in your success, or do they really want you to fail so they can keep you in the bucket with them? How large and generous are their visions? Remember that people with small visions of themselves cannot have a larger view of you.

You may not think it nice, but you owe it to yourself to separate from the "friends" who anchor you to a place where you do not wish to be.

There will always be people who try to knock you down. You don't need them in your life. There will always be people who attack your Big Idea. Don't dismiss what they have to say, but don't buy into it. Even if they seem to have the best intentions (they may think they're trying to protect you), your job is to listen to their arguments and use them as a counterbalance. See if there is anything they say that you can learn from and apply to your business or product in order to make it better. And if people say you're crazy and your Big Idea will never work, let their doubt drive you.

Your Fab Five

How important are the people you invest your time with? The time you spend with others is nothing less than precious—*and* an investment in your future.

My time with Tony Robbins taught me to look critically at the people around me. His circle included individuals who either were the very best at what they did or aspired to get there. This included people like Quincy Jones, Peter Guber, and Pat Riley. Among these top business leaders, world-class athletes, and people committed to changing the world were many others who had overcome big obstacles. They had found solutions that not only benefited themselves but also improved the lives of others along the way.

I'll never forget one member of Tony's circle, who had gotten in a car accident on the way to his wedding. The accident left him paralyzed from the waist down, but instead of feeling sorry for himself, he went out and invented a line of aerodynamic racing wheelchairs. He not only empowered himself but also helped others in the process.

During my time working for Tony's company, I assessed my own circle of friends and came to understand the power of our personal networks. What I learned was that I needed to recruit the right people into my life. In particular, I had to be aware of the five people I spent most of my time with. I call these five people the *Fab Five*.

The name "Fab Five" came into wide use in reference to what many people consider the greatest recruiting class in sports history, the 1991 Michigan men's basketball team. In their first year, these freshman players took their team to the NCAA championship, a remarkable and unprecedented accomplishment. In the same way Michigan's coach recruited them, you need to recruit and build your own championship team around you. Let's begin by looking at your existing Fab Five and considering their impact on you today.

Make a list of the five people you spend the most time with outside your family. If you're not sure whom to choose, just look at the last five numbers you dialed on your mobile phone. Now estimate what each of them earns, total the incomes, and divide by five. The number you end up with will be really close to what you earn. Crazy, right?

Maybe money isn't important to you, but another value is. Try the same exercise with your Fab Five's health status and their attitude toward the people around them (this time, if you wish, add your family to the list). Chances are you will get the same result.

Today you are nothing more—and nothing less—than the average of the five people you spend the most time with.

Ask yourself how your Fab Five affect you. Are they pulling you up or pushing you down? If you told your five best friends, one at a time, over coffee or a beer that you were planning to start a business, what would their responses be? Would they be supportive or dismissive? Would they encourage you or try to shoot your idea down? Would they be keen to help you brainstorm or would they turn the conversation back to themselves?

Are your Fab Five a reflection of your higher aspirations? This is important because we tend to hang around people whose values are similar to our own. Rich people hang out with rich people. Physically fit people hang out with physically fit people. And slobs hang out with slobs. If you want to know why you don't have more of the things you want in your life, the answer may be as close as the last five numbers you dialed on your mobile phone.

If you want to build a million-dollar business, you need to spend your time with people who have *already* built million-dollar businesses. If you want to build a ten-million-dollar business, you need to spend your time with people who have already built ten-million-dollar businesses. That's an important distinction, because the people who have built smaller companies won't know how to get you to the next level. Maybe you want to build a billion-dollar business but think you can't get to billionaires. That's no more than a convenient excuse. Pick up a book by Warren Buffett, follow Mark Cuban's blog, or attend live events with Tony Robbins.

Immerse yourself in the way your core group sees the world. Learn how they program their minds. Let their learning and instincts wash over you. If you spend enough time reading and absorbing their material, you will start to pick up how they act, think, and make decisions. Their state of mind will start to rub off on you.

You may not want to hear it or admit it, but you may have to change your circle of friends. If the people you spend the most time with cannot help you get to where you want to be, then you need to expand your network and make new friends. That doesn't mean that you have to abandon old friends, but the ecosystem of the entrepreneur needs a different balance. Finding success is a different pursuit from having fun, from recreational shopping for shoes or tailgating at the football game. The people you feel the most comfortable with—maybe the ones who demand the least— aren't necessarily the ones who'll move you toward your goals.

In order to move to the next level, you may need to add new people to your Fab Five—or create a new Fab Five from scratch. The people and thinking that got you this far are not going to take you where you want to go. If they could, you'd already be there.

THE PEOPLE AROUND YOU

Are the people around you pulling you up or holding you down?

Take Inventory: Write down the names of the five people you spend the most time with. Ask yourself: *Do they support me? Do they want to see me succeed in my new venture? Or would they prefer to see me fail and keep me close?* If the answer to that last question is yes, check them off your list and get them out of your life.

Find Three Mentors: Answer this question: Who are your three mentors? If you don't know, you'd better get to work finding one . . . and another . . . and another.

. . . .

Find Someone to Mentor: It's not enough to get guidance. You also need to give. I recommend that everyone mentor at least one person half his or her age. Interacting with students and younger entrepreneurs will give you an entirely fresh perspective and help you see things in a whole new way.

What Do Those Note Cards Say About You?

As an entrepreneur you must forge your own personal brand. As a manager in a big company, building a personal brand is just as important, because a strong brand will give you more power and influence within the organization. To put it another way, you must author your own story, paint your own portrait.

You may think you are selling a product, a financial plan, or something else to your investors, division heads, partners, or employees. And to be sure, those things may be part of the appeal. Yet it's really all about you, because people invest in people. Every action you take helps others define you. You may think you're saying nothing about yourself, but are really conveying everything there is to know about you.

I run a personal-branding exercise at one of my programs. Typically there are about twenty people in the room. On the first day I encourage the participants to mingle while grabbing coffee and breakfast before the event. When it's time to get started, they are invited to sit in their assigned seats. On the table in front of each of them is a placard. They are asked to print their names on the placards so everyone in the group can see. Each person is then handed a stack of index cards. I ask them to look around the room, write one person's name on each of their index cards, and jot down the first five words that come to mind when thinking of that person. An assistant then collects all the cards, enters all the words the group used to describe each participant into a file, and prints them out so that each participant sees only the words used to describe him or her.

People's reactions are amazing. Typically they are shocked, horrified, and very upset about the way others view them. For example, a person might think of himself as outgoing, but the index card shows the group thinks his behavior is obnoxious. Another person thinks she embodies the image of success and confidence, but the index cards indicate the group sees an arrogant and stand-offish person.

Often, the way others see us just doesn't sync with the story we've been telling ourselves about the image we think we are portraying. It's little wonder that we're not getting the results we want with our businesses in selling our ideas or raising capital. Clearly, what we are projecting is not what we need to win people over.

What would that stack of note cards say about you? What is the impression you are leaving on others? Is that personal brand serving you or stifling your growth? Is it taking you closer to or further away from your goals?

There are deliberate steps you can follow to take control of your personal brand.

Identify your goal. The first thing you need to do is get very clear about what it is you want to achieve. Do you want to take a consumer online business to market in ninety days? Do you want to release a new product that extends your company's footprint in the marketplace? Do you want to close financing for a big project? Do you want to create a rock-star team to help transform your local business into a global franchise?

Who do you need to be to achieve that goal? What image do you need to project to bring others along with you?

Understand where you are now. Where are you today relative to where you need to be? What is the gap, and what changes do you need to make to fill it?

To answer this question go to the five people you spend the most time with (your Fab Five) and ask them to use words to describe your brand. Then extend your pool to others with whom you have had fewer interactions; the more distant acquaintances may offer even more valuable impressions because they are based on more immediate first impressions. When you get a handle on how others see you, you'll have a better idea of what needs to change. If they say you're standoffish, when you've just thought of yourself as shy, this is an area of your self-presentation that you need to work on. Such knowledge alone can be curative.

Recognize what daily habits say about you. Do your habits empower or disempower you? What is the message your habits tell others about you? Daily habits can have a big impact on how people brand you. Your attire, manners, and degree of organization tell people about you—and the right presentation communicates that you came to play, you are prepared, and you have pride in who you are and what you do. For example, when someone is very physically fit and really takes care of himself, he presents as disciplined, committed, and apt to follow through. People can see and hear certain energy in their physical presence immediately. On the other hand, someone who does not take the same pride and care in his appearance sends a completely different message. Creating empowering habits based on higher standards is vital.

The biggest difference between where you are now and the place you want to be is the standard you set for yourself.

Little things make a big difference, even if it's just the cut of your suit or the warmth of your handshake—and you can take control of these factors. If you don't define who you want to be and manage your personal brand accordingly, people will do it for you. On the basis of the cues you give them, they will put you in a box. It's a box that best serves their needs and not yours, so make sure it's a box you want to be identified with.

Leverage technology to define and reinforce your brand. Most people will first be introduced to you online, when they type your name into Google or visit your LinkedIn, Facebook, or Twitter profile. They'll see the pictures and videos you distribute of yourself and what interests you. Use these tools to your advantage: Have a professional take your picture, inset a link to your Web site, and make sure your message is clear and your copy is brief and to the point.

Be yourself. Don't pretend to be someone else. When developing a personal brand in today's multimedia world, authenticity is key. If you try to pass yourself off as someone you are not, people will find out and that will undercut your credibility. Be original, be creative, but don't try to be what you think other people want you to be. Be the sincerest, most heightened version of yourself. When investors and customers meet you, you want them to think, *This is a person I want to do business with.*

If there are things from your career or past that you don't want to share or are afraid of how others will react to, don't hide them. Address them up front and, by doing so, take control of the conversation. For example, if an earlier business venture failed, don't try to hide it. Illuminate it by sharing what you learned from the experience and how you are applying those lessons going forward. Here's a secret: Most people would rather get behind people who took a shot, even if they failed. People who have learned from their mistakes bring wisdom to a new venture going forward.

Don't be defined by your origins. I'm a huge Los Angeles Lakers fan. One of my heroes growing up was Lakers owner Jerry Buss. He was a Depression-era baby who stood in food lines to eat, but he didn't let that experience define him. In college he saved $86 from each $750 paycheck he received, then got seven guys together and bought an apartment building. He built a real-estate empire, enabling him to buy the Los Angeles Lakers. Today he's an American icon, with a business worth at least one billion dollars. He wrote his own story and created his own brand. It is your job to do the same.

WRITE YOUR THIRTY-SECOND COMMERCIAL

You're selling yourself, and don't forget it. It is important to do it well, in clear and crisp fashion. Follow this simple formula whenever you are introduced to anyone (potential investors, partners, customers, tradespeople) in a business setting.

Tell Them Who You Are: Start with your name, your title, and a one-sentence description of what your company does.

Tell Them Whom You Serve: Compose a one-sentence description of your target customer. Be as specific as possible.

Share the Benefit: Describe how your customer will benefit from what you offer.

(continued on next page)

(continued from previous page)

Ask for the Order: At the end of your thirty-second pitch, ask whether the person you're talking to could benefit from or knows someone who could benefit from these services.

· ·

You can use this commercial even if someone casually asks you what you do. The more you practice your pitch, the clearer and more powerful it becomes.

Write Your Own Story

A great football season looked like it was about to crash and burn. The 1977 squad at the University of Arkansas, coached by Lou Holtz, had earned a berth in the Orange Bowl, and the Razorbacks were set to play their longtime rivals, the University of Oklahoma Sooners. The winner of the game was a virtual lock to take home the national championship. But bad things began to happen to Holtz's team. In one of the last practices before the game, Arkansas lost an All-American guard to injury. A couple days after that, Coach Holtz had to suspend both of his starting running backs and a wide receiver for disciplinary reasons.

The press jumped all over these developments, decreeing that Arkansas had no hope of beating the Sooners, who had won two of the last three national championships. Arkansas fell to being a twenty-four-point underdog. In his first season as head coach, Louis Leo Holtz looked like he was about to go from a leading candidate for coach of the year to goat of the year.

Many years later I worked an event where Holtz—who would go on to legendary success in eleven seasons at the University of

Notre Dame and later become a popular motivational speaker—told the story of how he and his team saved the season.

Holtz told us how he brought his team together in the locker room before the game. He began by acknowledging the situation they were in and the long odds they had been given by the experts. He told his ball club that everybody was trying to define them, to write their obituary before the first play was called (just as some people will try to do with your new business or product). Holtz pulled out a copy of the newspaper and held it up so everyone could read the boldface headline, which predicted a big loss for Arkansas.

"Everyone else has already decided who you are, what you will do, what the outcome of the game will be," said Holtz. "If you don't define yourself, others will do it for you."

With that, he folded the paper in half and ripped it. Then ripped the torn pages again. And then did it a third time.

Holding the wad of torn newspaper in his hand, he gave them his bottom line.

"Champions don't let others write their story," he said. "They write their own story."

With the ease of a practiced magician, he raised his arm as if to toss the shredded paper into the air. Instead of a shower of paper, however, the coach unfurled a fresh newspaper. This one had a different headline: ARKANSAS WINS. Which is exactly what his team did that day, soundly beating the Sooners 31–6.

The magic trick had just been an illusion, but Holtz's message is one every entrepreneur and intrapreneur should take to heart: Don't let anyone try to define you or tell you what you can or cannot do. As Holtz has said, "You can't let naysayers pull you down. Remember: If someone says you can't accomplish something, it is an opinion and nothing more. It is only a fact if you say it is."

Launching a successful new business, product, or service begins with having vision, letting go of your fear, and making the decision to move forward. It is followed by mitigating your risk every step of the way, so if things don't work out as planned, you have protected yourself and have the ability to bounce right back.

But it doesn't end there.

Your success or failure will be largely influenced by the impressions you make on others. It will also be impacted by your environment. This includes the people in whom you choose to invest your time.

Most important, your success during launch will depend on how you handle the ups and downs of entrepreneurship and how effective you are at smoothing out the ride. By asking better questions, you will be in the best possible position to succeed, no matter what life or business throws your way—and be headed toward making your dreams come true.

STAGE II.

FUELING THE TANK

*Thirty Days to Assemble
Your Resources*

CHAPTER 4.

BUSINESS PLANNING

If you can't explain it simply, you don't understand it well enough.
—ALBERT EINSTEIN

Biceps and Business

Entrepreneurs are by nature impatient people. Once they have an image of their big-picture objectives, many go from napkin to execution with nothing in the middle. They rush out and start executing without a plan.

While goals and objectives may give you a direction, they don't tell you what specific things you need to do to succeed. Although the strategies you use to accomplish your goals will evolve as you do business, the clearer you are from the start, the better a shot you have at building a winner.

My favorite example of the power of combining clear goals with a well-thought-out plan comes from my good friend Doug Brignole.

A few years ago I decided that I wanted to get really fit. The first thing I did was go to the gym and ask to be referred to a trainer. The guy they connected me with just wasn't what I wanted. Although he had muscle, he was also overweight and, worse yet, unhappy. He wasn't the kind of person I wanted to emulate. On the other hand, the man did make me realize that I should be modeling myself after someone who is the very best at what he does. So I made a decision: *I want to learn from Mr. Universe!* I put the word out to my friends, and that's how Doug entered my life.

Doug grew up in Southern California in a first-generation immigrant family. He was a small kid and he frequently got beaten up on his way home from grade school. At age fourteen he decided that he had had enough and that it was important to improve his physique. He went to a local gym and asked, "Can I *please* join?"

He was too young to be a member, but Doug persisted. He worked out an arrangement with the manager to work part time and work out during his off hours. He fell in love with bodybuilding and eventually got the urge to compete. By the time he was seventeen, he was a contender for Mr. Teen California. Though he didn't win that year, he did come in second, kicking off a lifelong career in bodybuilding. The rush of competing fueled him, so Doug set his goal higher: He wanted to become Mr. America.

Doug started by making sure he was absolutely clear on his outcome. He is not only a bodybuilder but also a world-class artist. One of his unique skills is his ability to draw the body and biomechanics in amazing detail.

Doug had a friend take a photo of him in a bodybuilder's pose, and Doug blew up the image. He put tracing paper on top of the enlargement and drew, in very fine detail, exactly what he would need to look like in order to win the title. He illustrated the shape, size, and balance of each muscle group as he projected it would be by the time the next contest rolled around.

Once Doug was absolutely clear on what he wanted, he asked himself the following questions: *What do I need to do to achieve it? What could get in the way? How am I going to overcome each challenge?*

This was years ago, before you could find twenty choices for protein powder at the store and smoothies on every corner. Like other professional bodybuilders at that time, Doug prepared all of his own meals, figuring out a dietary regimen that would enhance his workouts. He put that tracing-paper picture of himself in a frame and set it on the table where he ate five times a day. With every bite he took, he'd point his spoon or fork at the picture and say, *That's what I will look like.* And he'd take another bite. *I'm going to make that happen.* He did this for months.

From time to time Doug would have his friend take a new picture of him in the same pose, and then he would blow that up and lay the tracing of his goal body on top. In doing this, he took inventory and monitored his progress. He adjusted his diet and bodybuilding routine based on the results. Pound by pound, muscle by muscle, he filled out the image, bringing a dream, an idea sketched on tracing paper, to life.

Finally Doug competed and won the Mr. America title in his division.

After the competition, Doug had his friend take one final photograph. He posed just as he had in the original, so many months earlier. He blew the new picture up and laid the original tracing paper on top. The photo of Doug and the original image he had drawn of his goal were identical.

Doug Brignole set clear goals, created a solid plan, checked his results periodically, and made necessary adjustments. He executed in a similar fashion for his other goals as well, eventually winning the title of Mr. Universe. Though now in his fifties, Doug Brignole is still competing; recently he was the overall winner at the Muscle Beach International competition in the Masters Division.

Here's how we can all apply the lessons from Doug's story to turn our Big Ideas into a reality.

Be clear on what you want. Your goals must be specific, be measurable, and have deadlines. It's not enough to say, *I want to make one million dollars.* You need to be much more specific. *I want to earn one million dollars in net revenue by this specific date.* For your business, it's too vague to say, *I want to increase sales.* A better goal would be *I want to increase sales to one million dollars per quarter by a specific date with a specific profit margin.* Clarity is power. You can't manage what you can't measure.

Make a list of what you need to do. Clear goals are important, but you must back them up with a solid strategic plan. I heard recently that having clear goals increases an entrepreneur's chance of success by 20 percent. But having clear goals and combining them with a well-thought-out plan increases your chance of success by *400 percent.*

It's important to break down what is required to accomplish your goal into small, manageable pieces. When you're finished, ask yourself, *Is this it? If I do all these things, will it be enough? Will I reach my goal? Or are there other things I need to do?* Odds are, there are more steps than you realized.

Identify what could get in the way. To accomplish your goal of one million dollars in gross sales per quarter by a specific date with a specific profit margin, you may need to clear obstacles in your path. For example, you may need to tweak your product, refine your sales pitch, upgrade the people on your team, or find ways to reduce costs. Decide how you will overcome each roadblock. Make a list of everything you will need to do in order to break through each one.

Find models. Whom do you know who has already accomplished the same goal successfully? Model your plan on what has worked for them, and learn from what didn't.

Having a Big Idea is a good start, but it's not enough to be successful. You need clear goals that are specific, are measurable, and have deadlines. You need a plan in place that tells you what you need to achieve, what could get in the way, and how you will overcome each obstacle. By combining your Big Idea with clear goals and a strategic plan, you put yourself on the right course to bring your idea to life in the next ninety days.

Start with the Last Page First

What is the first step in getting clear on how to execute your Big Idea? Creating a working model for your business.

We've all been brainwashed into thinking that the best way to do this is to sit behind our desks and write a long, detailed business plan. You know the kind. It starts with a fancy cover and your mission statement and then describes your team, market, product, and competition and the rest of the elements.

Most entrepreneurs spend a lot of time and resources writing their plan. Too often they get feedback during the process from all the wrong people. This includes their friends, their family, and others who want to support them. The problem is, most of these people will tell the entrepreneurs only what they want to hear— that they have come up with the next Google or Apple or Tesla (keep in mind, none of this feedback is coming from customers). By the time the entrepreneur gets to the last section in the business plan—the financial section—he's totally sold on the idea. So he decides to leave the financial section of the plan unfinished or drop it altogether and start executing.

Intrapreneurs face an equally dangerous problem: the temptation to take a basic set of assumptions and artificially blow up the numbers to make the business look more attractive and ultimately get the support needed to move forward.

And why not? We are passionate. We are committed. We know we can't fail. So what are we waiting for? *Let's go!*

Here's the problem. I've found that most entrepreneurs change their business model about six times when working through the financial section of their plans. While running the numbers, they identify key distinctions with regard to income and expenses. They gain a deeper understanding of what it will take to break even and how to build cash flow. As a result, they are able to come up with better-informed strategies for attaining the desired financial outcomes.

The most important part of the initial business-planning process, and the one that people most often neglect, involves getting your numbers to tell a story that makes good sense for you and your investors. If you start at the beginning of the plan, then get to the end only to learn that your assumptions about the business and your plan to execute don't pan out, you will need to start over. In the meantime, you've lost valuable time and money.

In our three-month time frame to launch, we don't have the time for you to make that mistake. Here's what I recommend.

Start with the last page first. Once I have a basic understanding of what I'd like to build, I dig right into the numbers. I create a simple one-page spreadsheet that clearly identifies how the money flows. Basically, I write business plans backward. What I have learned is that once you nail a financial model where the numbers tell the story you want, the rest of the plan will write itself.

Don't wait. Don't make this process more difficult than it needs to be. Limit your model to one page. Create the simplest, most basic spreadsheet you can that projects income, expenses, breakeven, cash flow, and the capital required to achieve your outcome. Use conservative assumptions and do not rely on best-case scenarios.

Get out of the office. You will learn more about your business by getting into the market than you ever will sitting behind a desk. At least 50 percent of your time should be spent outside the office gathering information that can be applied to your plan. That means getting in front of industry insiders to learn more about the market, talking to prospects about their needs, and testing your competition's products and services.

Be careful whom you listen to. When we have an idea we passionately believe in, we are convincing. It's easy for our family and friends to say what we want to hear and tell us we have a winner on our hands because they want to be supportive. But when modeling your business, don't focus on the feedback you get from the people closest to you. The people whose feedback matters the most are current and potential customers. Listen to what they have to say. Apply what you learn to your model. Let their direct feedback and not your enthusiasm sway your projections.

Don't throw out negative feedback. Sometimes it's difficult for entrepreneurs to listen to negative feedback. Usually they are so close to their projects and have so much on the line, they don't want to hear that their assumptions may be wrong. As a result, they start rejecting, deflecting, and pushing aside feedback that isn't in line with what they believe, instead of using that feedback to their advantage. Honest and educated feedback is like gold. Use it to open up your mind and ask tough questions about your assumptions. You must be obsessively committed to taking in this feedback and asking what you can learn from it and how you can apply it.

This is especially important for people entering new markets where they don't have prior experience. Getting feedback from others who have lived in the space will add to your perspective.

Sometimes you will learn that there are things that you can't see as a newcomer that would significantly impact your financial results.

Be open to what the numbers tell you. The worst thing that you can do is try to manipulate a model to match your initial assumptions. You need to approach your financial model with a completely open mind. Recognize that it will probably take longer than you initially thought to get to market, generate revenues, create profits, and accumulate the cash you need to further invest in the business. The odds are that, by being open, you will be able to make good decisions, apply them to your business, and set yourself on a path to success.

The One-Page Plan

If we're going to market in ninety days, we simply don't have time for a ninety-page plan. I like beautiful charts and graphs as much as the next entrepreneur, but frankly, we don't have the bandwidth to focus on that much information—and neither do your potential investors, partners, and team members. As President Ronald Reagan used to tell his staff, "Give me everything I need to know, but keep it to one page."

Once you've created a sound financial model, what you need to top it off is a one-page "executive summary" that clearly describes your business.

An executive summary is one of the most valuable tools for both entrepreneurs and managers inside big organizations. It should highlight the company's or project's team, mission, market served, target customer, problem being solved, unique value proposition, competitive environment, financial assumptions, exit strategy, and return on investment.

This document should be clear and easy to read. The executive summary should be shared with your team to ensure that everyone in your fast-moving start-up is headed in the same direction. This summary can also be given to potential investors, partners, and customers to draw interest. And yes, you do need to keep it all on one page.

Many people have said to me, "But I need more space!" My response? "If you can't explain what you want to do in a few sentences, then you don't really understand your business." And by the way, nobody else will, either.

I didn't say this would be easy. In fact, when you ask most entrepreneurs to summarize their business in a sentence, on a single page, or in a PowerPoint deck, they can't do it. Instead they ramble on and on. In the real world, giving potential investors too much is the same as giving them nothing at all. They'll throw your plan right in the trash.

That's why this tool is so valuable. It provides focus for you, your team, and anyone else who touches the business. When you get in front of your target investor, you will be prepared and you will be different. In today's world, that's what you need to stand out and get the deal done.

An Expensive Hobby

Even before launch, you need to plot an exit strategy. It's a very important step that too many founders skip. They either are too eager to get started, firmly believe they would never sell, or are concerned that focusing on an exit so early in the company's life cycle would just be a distraction. Let me give you three reasons why *now* is the right time to begin thinking about an exit.

First, your investors want to know how they will make money and get a good return on their investment. Will it be from an IPO or sale? If your plan is to sell, who will buy you? Why will they buy your business? How will they value the company? Can you point to comparable purchases to support your case?

Second, planning an exit will provide a logical way for you to think strategically about your business. For example, what does your target buyer need that your business can provide (such as sales, new customers, new products, or new markets)? What metrics would they use when evaluating the strength of your business, such as revenue, gross profit, net profit, or EBITA (earnings before interest, taxes, and amortization)? Who in those organizations buys companies, and how can you be proactive and build relationships? The answers to these questions could have a big impact on the company in terms of its plans, partnerships, and overall strategy.

Third, at some point you may just need or want to get out. Even if you self-finance or think you will never sell, many reasons could surface that change your thinking. You may at some point decide it's time to cash out. You may feel burned out or just get the urge to do something else. Sometimes business goes sideways or a major change in your personal life makes a quick sale necessary. As a result, I recommend that entrepreneurs have at least two escape hatches or exit scenarios planned in the event they need them.

Finally, consider this: A business without an exit plan is an incredibly expensive hobby. If you're looking to do something for escape or relaxation, starting a new business is not the right move. I recommend fishing instead.

Below are a few ideas to consider when thinking through your exit strategy in the early days of your business. They can be—and should be—considered simultaneously with your launch.

Create deep relationships. Businesses are bought and not sold. The best acquisitions at the highest returns typically come as the result of long-standing relationships or strategic partnerships. These give buyers the opportunity to get to know you and your business and you the opportunity to sell yourself to them.

Keep your house in order. You should always keep your financials and other business documents up to date and filed in an organized manner. When the time comes to sell, you will need clean financials to attract buyers and the highest valuations. If your back office runs well, that will instill confidence and make the selling process move faster. Plan and execute from the beginning.

Get back to work! Now that we've had this conversation, stop focusing on your billion-dollar exit and put all your energy back into focusing on serving your customer. Go build a great business and the rest will fall right into place.

Not Every Problem Is Made to Be Solved

Like many entrepreneurs, I constantly survey the landscape and keep my eye out for opportunities. A few years ago I spotted one. At least I thought I did.

Having made some good money in my Silicon Valley years, I wanted to reinvest part of my capital into something that would generate passive income. The answer, my new Big Idea, was *self-storage.*

I did some homework and found there were about forty thousand self-storage facilities in the United States. But the key fact that really got me excited was that the biggest owner, Public Storage, controlled just *3 percent* of the market. To me this spelled opportunity, the chance to develop a national brand, roll up the market through acquisitions, and create efficiencies through scale.

It didn't quite work out that way. Instead, I learned an important lesson: If a problem looks obvious but hasn't yet been solved, there may be a good reason. In the case of self-storage, the problem proved to be that 95 percent of the self-storage facilities were mom-and-pop businesses. These family operations typically consisted of only one facility, and often the owners lived on the premises. At some their kids worked the storefront. Why would they sell if their whole way of life revolved around the business? If they could be persuaded to sell, how hard would it be to get them to make the decision?

Another problem surfaced too. Once you get the couple who owns the business to move away, you're faced with a new challenge, because then you need to hire someone else to manage and watch the business. You also need to pay that person, an expense that the mom-and-pop managers didn't have because they were operating it themselves. The level of effort, time, and money it would have taken me to acquire hundreds, if not thousands, of family businesses and then rebrand them just didn't make business sense. I could spend a fraction of the energy it would take in another business and likely have better results.

After investing lots of time and money working on what I had thought was an obvious winner, I realized that because of my lack of experience in the industry, I hadn't understood certain mechanics of the business.

This doesn't mean there were not opportunities to build great companies in self-storage. The people who had succeeded already knew that you could not grow quickly through acquisition, so they had developed portfolios from the ground up and worked to build regional rather than national brands. When one of their portfolios came up for sale, they were prime targets for acquisition with very high values.

There's a larger conclusion to be reached from this experience too, one that you should consider. For generations entrepreneurs have fallen into the trap of thinking that all businesses and industries are pretty much the same. Some think that just because they've been successful in one industry, it will be easy to duplicate their success in a new industry, that one model suits all.

That can be true, of course, but never forget that every industry has its own character and that business cycles change. No two moments nor any two opportunities are identical. No matter how much you think you know or how good your business acumen, *always* walk into a new industry with a beginner's mind: open to learn. Do your homework and talk to lots of people before you plunge in. That means talking with people who are very close to the industry to help you understand the nuances of that particular business. It means poring over every piece of material you can find in a search for other companies that either are executing or have attempted to execute the model you are contemplating.

If you find there is a high failure rate, don't fool yourself into thinking your model is that much different or your team is that much smarter than others. Instead pause, take a deep breath, and learn everything you can about the companies that came before you.

You should also allow other people to weigh in on your plan, provided they have the background and experience to be worthy advisers. Be conscious of the difference between *opinion* and *counsel*. Opinions come from people who have no firsthand knowledge of something. Counsel comes from people who have direct personal experience in the area where you need guidance. Sound business planning requires input from the latter. Finally, take a good look at your timing. I've learned that it's better to have a terrible idea in a good market than a great idea at the wrong time.

Not all business problems are made to be solved. If you look at a market, see a problem, and conceive of a great solution, there may just be a good reason nobody else has "solved it." There could be something about the market or the specific industry that makes it a poor fit for what you want to introduce. That possibility makes doing your market research more than a matter of reading a book or a report. It means getting away from your desk and talking to people in the industry. It's seeking expert counsel every step of the way. Coming into an unfamiliar industry with fresh eyes can sometimes work—there's no question about that—especially if you're seeking to apply new technology to an old business. But beware: You may end up paying a high price to educate yourself.

Entrepreneurs can't take shortcuts. You need to build a solid plan, strategy, and financial model that support your goals. You need to do this *before* you start building your new business, product, or service. This critical step will help to mitigate risk. Unfortunately, too many entrepreneurs, in their excitement to get started, skip right over the planning stage. The business gets off on the wrong foot, and they have to go back and correct all their mistakes, which costs them valuable time and money.

Remember, the best shortcut is taking a long-term view.

CHAPTER 5.

SECURING YOUR CREW

Five guys working on the court together can achieve more than
five talented individuals who come and go as individuals.

—KAREEM ABDUL JABBAR

Broke or Billions?

Two friends of mine, born in the same place, work in the fashion
industry. Over the years, each has gained access to very similar
resources. Both have charismatic personalities and are natural
leaders. Yet one of these women constantly struggles—her business is broke and may have to close its doors—while the other's is
now worth over a billion dollars.

The obvious question: With so much in common, what's the
difference?

The short answer is that the successful entrepreneur had great
self-awareness. She recognized early on what she did well and,
just as important, where she needed help. She knew from the start
to build a team with the right skills around her and then to get out

of their way. This strategy allowed her to work her strengths and to hire her weaknesses. Her key tactic—and it's a good one—is to find people who *play* doing the things she considers *work*.

In effect, she fired herself as CEO, putting in place someone else with a track record of successfully building companies like the one she wanted to create. This allowed her to focus on product development, the work she does best and enjoys most. The company thrived.

In contrast, the struggling entrepreneur did two things wrong. First, she tried to do everything she could herself, from scheduling meetings to going on sales calls to making the product and shipping it to her customers. She was always so busy working *in* the business that she had no time to do work *on* the business. Second, she put herself in the wrong role. Although she too was miscast as a CEO, she didn't have the insight to hand off the executive responsibilities.

An important element of a successful launch is to build the right team around you. What do you need to know about yourself and your potential crew to get you from idea to market in ninety days?

Work your strengths; hire your weaknesses. One of the best qualities an entrepreneur can exhibit is self-awareness. Know yourself. Are you a visionary? Do you like to take risks? Are you better at setting up systems and managing day-to-day operations than at thinking big? Is there a specific skill (such as sales, marketing, or product development) where you excel? Get clear about who you are and how you can help the organization most, and then focus on filling the gaps by putting the right people around you.

Sometimes entrepreneurs, perhaps out of pride, find it difficult to put someone else in the role of CEO. The same hesitation may also apply to other leadership roles. My advice? *Get over it.* This kind of limited thinking will only obstruct your path to your success.

Aim to hire people more qualified and smarter than you are in functional areas, and give them the tools they need to succeed. By the way, assigning somebody else a major role in the company doesn't mean you have to give up your influence in or ownership of the company. When your role is in perfect alignment with who you are, you will be able to contribute more and really enjoy what you are doing in the process.

Look at the histories of other companies. The most successful ones were typically started by people who brought in others very early in the companies' life cycles to raise their performance.

When Sara Blakely got started, she worked on Spanx at night, filling orders from home and personally going into stores to rearrange product displays. Later, as the business grew, she recognized that at heart she's a visionary rather than a CEO. So she hired a woman with ten years of experience running a licensing division at Coca-Cola to run day-to-day operations at Spanx. She played to her strengths, hiring to cover her weaknesses.

Sergey Brin and Larry Page, the creative geniuses behind Google, fired themselves as CEOs and hired an experienced executive, Eric Schmidt, to run the company. Schmidt helped engineer its exponential growth while Brin and Page kept doing what they did best.

Be ready to substitute players. As a company grows, people who excelled early on may no longer be the right fit. One manager may be great at taking a product to market but not seem to know how to grow the business beyond a certain point. I've seen people who perform brilliantly at one level but don't know how to shift gears to get the company to the next one; they're great at taking a business to a million or even ten million dollars in sales, but not to a hundred. That's not surprising, because a different set of skills is required to get the company to each new level. It's your job to make sure you always have the right people in the right places at the right time in your company's life cycle.

At launch one key thing to consider is that employees, partners, and contractors need to be comfortable working in fast-paced, resource-constrained environments where they will likely be asked to juggle multiple tasks. Also, because launching is so time consuming, you must be sure the people on your team do not have any other major obligations during the critical go-to-market period.

Bring in the right people, give them all the tools they need to succeed, and then get out of their way. Leverage your strengths and spend your days doing the work you enjoy most. This could be the difference between going broke and building a billion-dollar business.

HOW CAN YOU CONTRIBUTE MOST TO YOUR COMPANY?

The first step in building a great team is having a clear understanding of your strengths and weaknesses and then filling in the gaps. In other words, fire yourself from a job that does not fit you best and rehire yourself in a position where you can contribute most. Which label below best describes you?

. . . .

Visionary: You love dreaming big and getting people inspired, but you're just not passionate about taking risk and being in charge of the day-to-day execution. If this sounds familiar, you should look for someone who can bring your vision to life.

. . . .

Entrepreneur: You are a risk taker. You have vision, you think big, but you also like the idea of rolling up your sleeves and building a business. You thrive in fast-paced environments and like handling multiple responsibilities. You're comfortable with limited resources and can multitask like crazy.

Manager: You are not a wild-eyed visionary and you don't want to take on all that risk. You like to add structure to an organization in order to achieve its goals. You enjoy overseeing a team, building systems and best practices. You pay attention to data, details, and key business metrics. You feel most comfortable in a more stable environment and when executing.

Sharpshooter: You have a craft, a unique skill, or a basic knack for doing great things in a particular area. Perhaps you are an artist or salesperson. Do you excel at writing code? Have you mastered a skill that you just love to exercise? You may be less interested in being a CEO or manager because it would get in the way of your working on the things you enjoy most.

Your Role as Flight Commander

I often ask entrepreneur CEOs and corporate managers the following question: What is your responsibility as the person in charge of running your business?

This is often met with a blank stare. Other times I get a vague response, something like, "Well, I do a lot of things. I guess my job is to keep the company or project moving forward."

Those are not useful answers. It's no wonder that many entrepreneur CEOs just wander from one crisis to the next without any real thought about how to proactively drive the company forward.

Before you assemble your team, the first thing you must do is get absolutely clear on what your role and day-to-day responsibilities will be leading the company. You need to figure this out early. Knowing what to focus on will also help ensure you're not spending your time in other people's business and getting in the way of their doing their jobs.

Every CEO is different, but that doesn't mean we can't learn from the best. That brings me to my old friend Mark Moses. He is the entrepreneur CEO that I look up to most.

Mark is just a little bit competitive. On personality tests he rates as a "super achiever." His life story reinforces the picture. Driven to succeed no matter the cost, he founded several successful companies; the last one, Platinum Capital, became a billion-dollar business. Then, after "retiring" at the ripe old age of forty, he threw himself into Ironman triathlons. He's competed in eleven of those, even breaking the eleven-hour mark, which is pretty awesome for the Ironman distance.

But let's go back in time. As a college kid in Canada, he started a company called Student Painters. In his *first summer* with the business, Mark did $70,000 in sales and made an $18,000 profit, impressive indeed in an era when college tuition topped out around $5,000. The next summer he did $120,000 in sales and cleared $35,000. "I thought maybe I didn't want to be an accountant after all," Mark remembers.

Mark knew his results were good, but he decided to see what would happen if he went out and hired talented people, taught them how to model the system he'd built, and helped them to grow prosperous businesses for themselves. In return he would get a small cut. With that in mind, he packed up a U-Haul and headed for California. There he eventually grew Student Painters to 250 branches with three thousand guys and gals armed with paint brushes. I was one of those painters. I became friends with Mark as a college freshman when I opened a branch for him in San Diego.

After four years in the business, he sold Student Painters for millions of dollars. Next Mark went into the mortgage-banking business. He kept building the business, but in 1997 he set himself—and his company, Platinum Capital—a new goal of lifting sales over a billion dollars. To kick off the crusade he rented a two-ton elephant and rode it into the annual company meeting. He told his people, "If we think big and act big, we will be big. Let's do a billion dollars!"

Overnight the elephant became—and remained—the symbol of the company. The very next day employees started bringing in elephant objects: paperweights, pictures, posters, and stuffed animals. By creating and reinforcing this shared vision, Mark created a rock-star culture. "People knew us as the elephant company," Mark says. "I was the elephant guy."

But Mark's ride in the mortgage business turned out to exemplify the ups and downs of entrepreneurship that every one of us faces. In 1998, when the Asian flu hit and lending dried up overnight, Mark was forced to lay off 230 employees. In 2000 his business was a day away from bankruptcy, until an angel investor stepped in and loaned the company the necessary capital it needed to keep its doors open. Mark then turned the company around, building a $1.6 billion, 550-employee business. Finally, in 2006, he sold Platinum Capital. Today Mark is a coach for CEOs and entrepreneurs. He teaches them how to figure out where they want to go, helps them build a plan to get there, and holds them accountable for execution along the way.

What I particularly respect about Mark is his ability to cut through the garbage and tell it like it is. One concept he works really hard to teach his CEO clients is the central role of the entrepreneur CEO. Having run and invested in quite a few businesses ranging from a painting company to a large lender, his view may be surprising to you: He sees the job of the leader as very similar, whatever the business.

Being the head decision maker is just the start. With a thank-you to Mark, then, I want to share some of the most important parts of your day-to-day job description.

The CEO is responsible for the vision and the direction of the company. This seems straightforward enough, but it's more complicated than it sounds. When I ask CEOs where their company will be three years from now, fewer than one in ten has a good answer. This is inexcusable.

You have to look at the horizon and know where you want to take your company. This kind of vision differs from a goal on your mission statement; your vision is a measurable three-, five-, or ten-year view of where you want to be. I recommend starting with the sales and profits you hope to achieve and then working backward to see what it will take to make those happen. You need clear drivers, processes, and a form of accountability to manage your company's progress toward your vision. In short, having a vision is pretty worthless unless you engineer the specifics to achieve it.

The CEO has the ultimate responsibility for cash. Wait, you ask, isn't watching the cash the job of the CFO, accountant, or bookkeeper? No.

For any company, cash and access to cash are the lifeblood, the air you breathe. If you run out of cash, you're done. You'd be surprised at how even a company with high profit margins that is growing quickly can run short of cash. The reason for this, says Mark Moses, is that "growth eats cash." You may have to use up cash to add to your working capital or to build up inventory or to finance your accounts receivable. Managing the monetary ebb and flow is ultimately the CEO's responsibility because it is so vital to the health and survival of the business.

The CEO must ensure that the right people are in the right jobs at the right time. "Lots of CEOs fall down on this one," says

Mark. CEOs may be sentimentally attached to old employees who have been there from the beginning. They refuse to think of letting them go or moving them aside, even if their time of usefulness has passed.

As the business grows, needs change. The people who got you to one threshold may not be the people you need to take you to the next level. The CEO, hard-hearted though it may seem, has to be dispassionate about hiring and firing. If you can afford only two salespeople, they need to be the two best salespeople you can afford. Some people operate better in start-ups than in more mature environments. Recognize your people's strengths and weaknesses, and don't wait too long to bring in new talent. The wrong people will bring you down.

The CEO is responsible for key relationships. The CEO has to "own" the key relationships in the company, such as those with bankers, key vendors, the most important customers, and shareholders. Any outsider who wields the power to alter the future of your company—by ordering, selling, lending, whatever—needs access to you (and you to them). You want them to be comfortable calling you up at any hour of the day or night. This is very important because too often business owners hand over these relationships to key employees. But what happens if your employees leave and try to take those accounts with them? You cannot—and should not—keep control of every contact. But know who the key ones are and keep them close.

The CEO must have processes in place to continue learning. You did your market research before you started your company, right? Back then you didn't have anything invested. You had nothing on the line. But now that your life and future are tied up in your enterprise, be diligent about keeping up with happenings in your industry, with your competitors, and with your customers.

Circumstances change faster than ever these days, and the annals of recent corporate history are littered with the bones of companies that didn't evolve or adapt fast enough to get out of the way of change. Go to conferences, talk to consultants, and get to know your rivals. Use tools like Google Alerts and LinkedIn to automatically get news of what's happening in your field and outside it. Read trade blogs and e-zines. Look to learn—as well as sell—when you're out there, whether it's one on one or at a convention with thousands. Hire a business coach and put together an advisory board to gain experience from those who can help you.

The CEO must be a cheerleader. "The CEO has to be the chief energizing officer," says Mark. He or she must communicate what's going on to the rest of the team, explaining the company's results and getting employees on board with the vision for the future. "If you want them to buy in to what you're selling, then you have to align their best interests with your best interests," Mark insists. Often the best way to do that, he recommends, is through open and engaging communication.

Do you fit the CEO profile? Is this the kind of role you're prepared to play in your company? Are these the things you excel at? In the following pages we'll talk about finding out who you are and what the best role is for you in the business—so you can maximize results and love going to work every day.

• • •

THE COMMANDER'S CHECKLIST

Vision: Do you have a clear, specific, and measurable vision?

. . . .

Responsible for the Cash: You can't leave this task entirely to your CFO, accountant, or bookkeeper. It's too important to the company. Always keep an eye on your company's cash.

. . . .

People: You must make sure you have the right people in the right positions at the right times.

. . . .

Key Relationships: What happens if the person you hired to oversee accounts leaves? She probably takes that key relationship with her. You need to own the relationships that are most important to your business.

. . . .

Learning: Work at growing and educating your team. Also, stay on top of the market, competition, and customer needs.

. . . .

Cheerleader: Don't forget, you are the chief energizing officer!

Three Plays

Now that you've identified the role you will play in your business, the time has come to think about filling in the gaps. Identifying the best players, assigning them to the right positions, and making sure they clearly understand and excel in their roles are critical steps. They're what separate championship organizations from everyone else.

In the world of the National Football League, Stephen Austin is regarded as the expert of experts, a great evaluator of talent. Over twenty years he built his company, Elite Football Services, into the leading private evaluator of football players in the world. (In 2011, after several hundred players vetted by Austin had been signed with NFL teams, the National Football League bought EFS, making it the league's nationwide producer of combine showcase events.) Stephen's systems are so effective that they have been emulated by the top sports organizations all over the world. The U.S. Navy SEALs have even enlisted his help in finding the next generation of supreme warriors.

I asked Stephen, "What is it that separates the best players in the world from everyone else? What is the difference between players like Tom Brady, Jerry Rice, Dick Butkus and everyone else?" His answer surprised me.

It all comes down to this, he said: "Three plays."

That's it.

Three plays per game, the three moments in which a superstar does something just a little different from everyone else.

For a quarterback like Tom Brady, one of those things might be avoiding a sack. Another could be throwing the ball away instead of risking an interception. The third might be drawing an opposing linebacker offside with a change in cadence. Three things—often three little things—may not seem like a lot, but multiply those three plays per game times sixteen regular-season games, four play-off matchups, and a Super Bowl. That's *sixty-three* plays a year that the other guy, also a really talented player, didn't make.

Stephen explains that you can't tell if a person will make those three plays based on how he performs at the combine. (That means your organization must do its homework.) That's why Stephen's pro scouts watch hours and hours of game tape to understand how their candidate has performed in the past. They spend time getting to really know a player before making a decision to select him, talking to former coaches and teammates, collecting references. Investing the time to gather this kind of intelligence up front is one of the hallmarks of championship organizations.

I've found that one of the biggest mistakes busy entrepreneurs make is failing to invest enough time in learning about job candidates before making the decision to hire someone. Many soon learn that one or two bad hires can really set them back. Finding the right people takes time, but probably half as much time as it takes to unravel the mess that can come with hiring the wrong person, bringing in a replacement, and getting the company back on track. Since you want to find those teammates who can make critical plays for you, here are some steps for hiring well.

Get clear on what you need. With only ninety days to launch, you don't have time to waste. So begin with a very clear job description. This will save you more time and energy than anything else and will help produce the best results. The description should include the title, a list of responsibilities, the prior experience required, the functional expertise needed, educational requirements, and how much you're willing to pay (being transparent about money is important to avoid wasting time). The more detailed the profile, the easier you will find it to connect with the person you are looking for. Also, the easier it will be for your network to help you identify the right candidates.

From time to time you will need to fill a position for which you don't necessarily know all the day-to-day responsibilities or requirements. When this occurs, most entrepreneurs just try to wing it. Since that typically leads to a company's worst hires, I recommend you take a different approach.

For example, I once needed to hire someone in finance but I wasn't really sure what title, day-to-day job description, and background best fit my needs. I just knew I needed stuff done, so I reached out to a friend whose job it was to recruit people to fill financial positions in big companies. I shared with her what my business needed. She started by mapping out a finance department's organizational chart. She slotted in positions, including a chief financial officer, vice president, controller, accountant, and bookkeeper. She then provided me with sample job descriptions for each one and overviews of their day-to-day responsibilities, what kind of background I should be looking for in each, and the appropriate stages and times to bring them into my company. What I learned from the experience was that I really needed a controller, so we refined that job description and tailored it to my business, and I sent it out to my network. We made the right hire.

Where should you start looking for help when making key hires? I recommend talking to board members, investors, and other advisers to begin getting a feel for the position. Next, talk to people in your network already serving in the role you plan to hire. Ideally, they work for companies of similar size and at the same stage. Ask them about their roles, their responsibilities, and how they interact with management and their peers. These people can also offer you valuable referrals.

Don't talk to just anybody. When you complete your job description and résumés start coming in, make choices. Consider only the people who meet all your important requirements. Especially in the first ninety days, you don't have the time, and your investors won't have the patience, for on-the-job training.

Test, test, test. Take the time to really get to know your candidates. Do they match the job description? What do former employers, coworkers, and customers say about them? Have you and you team spent time with them both inside and outside the office?

Identify fast, test slow. When possible, start the person as an independent contractor instead of a full-time employee. This is a great opportunity to see the person in action and to watch how he or she works with your team. You can ensure that the fit is right before pulling the trigger to give him or her a full-time job. If it's not possible to start the person as a contractor (he or she is employed full time someplace else, for example), give him or her a simple assignment or project to complete during the interview process. It will help you and your team to understand how the person thinks and executes.

Never settle. If you do make the hire and it just doesn't work out, get rid of the person as fast as you can and move on with your business. There are plenty of great people out there. Be patient and wait to get the right one.

HIRE A BUSINESS COACH

Your Secret Weapon: Google CEO Eric Schmidt told *Fortune* magazine that the best business advice he ever got was to hire a coach. A coach is someone who brings out your best by providing counsel, support, feedback, and advice. "I initially resented the advice, because after all, I was a CEO," said Schmidt. "I was pretty experienced. Why would I need a coach? Am I doing something wrong? My argument was, How could a coach advise me if I'm the best person in the world at this? But that's not what a coach does. The coach doesn't have to play the sport as well as you do. They have to watch you and get you to be your best."

Don't Reinvent the Wheel: Remember, there are two paths to success: You can figure it out on your own through trial and error, wasting valuable time and money. Or you can find coaches and role models and advisers who have walked this path already and can show you the way.

The Perfect Marriage?

Think of the greatest partnerships of our time: Lennon and Mc-Cartney. Jobs and Wozniak. Gates and Allen. Ben and Jerry. Jagger and Richards. Hewlett and Packard. Half ended in divorce. Half lasted a lifetime.

A business partnership is a lot like a marriage. It's an everyday commitment, and in the early stages of a new venture you will probably spend more time with your business partner than with anyone else.

Potentially the most important decision you will make in these early days is whether or not to bring in partners to be coowners alongside you. If you do choose to go that route, you need to give as much thought to whom you take on as a business partner as you did to whether or not to marry your spouse. It's that big a deal.

Some partners seem to have been made for each other.

A man named Irv Robbins grew up working in his father's ice-cream shop. Irv's brother-in-law, Burton Baskin, also knew ice cream pretty well; he had enjoyed making it for the troops while serving as a lieutenant in the navy during World War II.

After the war, Robbins started Snowbird Ice Cream in Glendale, California. Baskin, who had married Robbins's sister Shirley before the war, ran a menswear shop in Chicago. When he and Shirley moved to LA, Robbins convinced Baskin that selling ice cream would be more fun than selling clothes. Baskin agreed and decided to open his own ice-cream store.

As Robbins once told a newspaper reporter: "I was about to sign a lease on a store in Pasadena, and I said, 'You take it. You go into the ice cream business and do the same thing I'm doing. And as soon as we have enough stores open, we can open up a little ice cream factory.'"

So two people in the same family opened two ice-cream stores in the same neighborhood. They decided to compete rather than becoming partners because both felt that if, as capable entrepreneurs, they joined forces, the compromises required of a joint business venture might get in the way of their creative ideas.

Over the next few years, however, as each built a successful business, Baskin and Robbins started to recognize that there might be significant benefits in banding together rather than competing against each other. They shared a similar vision. They agreed wholeheartedly to sell nothing but ice cream but make lots of different flavors. They also realized they had complementary skill sets, as one excelled in operations and the other in sales and marketing. They both had unique business networks that, put together, would enable them to reach out further and faster when trying to grow.

They decided to become business partners in their new ice-cream venture and selected the order of the names of their new company, Baskin-Robbins, with a coin toss.

They also created one of the great retail concepts of the past century: franchising. Because they both were well versed in what it meant to operate a store and understood the pride of ownership, they determined that the best way to grow was to find managers who wanted to buy a piece of the business. Baskin-Robbins became what is believed to be the first restaurant chain to franchise its outlets. Within five years it had forty shops in Southern California; soon after, it trademarked its 31 Flavors concept. Today Baskin-Robbins has more than 2,800 shops in the United States and 5,000 worldwide.

There's no single model for partnerships, but the Baskin-Robbins story is a great example of how, with a shared vision, similar temperaments, complementary skill sets, nonoverlapping networks, and hard work, partnerships can succeed.

In you're thinking about seeking a partner to join in your business, be sure to consider these issues:

Vision. You and your partner must share a common vision. You need to be on the same page, running in the same direction and toward the same goal.

Temperament. Oftentimes one partner is a natural leader while the other is more of a functional expert. New enterprises require a balance of both energies.

Complementary skill sets. Each partner should be able to make a unique contribution to the business. This will help the new venture to move further faster and with less capital required.

Complementary skill sets are also important because they help create clarity with regard to roles and responsibilities. For example, a great salesperson together with a great Web developer could make a powerful combination. But let's say a business is started by two powerhouse marketing experts. Odds are they will argue over roles, responsibilities, and decision-making power because their skills overlap.

Finally, investors prefer to see founding teams with two to three people who each bring something different to the table. Otherwise they feel like they are spending their money to pay for the same position twice.

Nonoverlapping networks. Each partner should have a unique network of relationships that the company can draw upon.

• • •

PUT IT ON PAPER NOW!

Like marriage, not all partnerships work out: Many end in divorce. That makes the business equivalent of a prenuptial agreement essential. It must be in writing and reviewed by your attorneys. At the very least it should address the following issues:

. . . .

Ownership: Who owns what percentage of the company's equity?

. . . .

Financial Commitment: What will each one of you put into the company? If more capital is needed, what's expected of each of you? Is the company financially responsible for contracts and accounts, or are you responsible as individuals?

. . . .

Time Commitment: How much time and effort will each side give to the company? If you're not expected to give evenly of your time and effort, then adjustments should be made in terms of ownership and compensation.

. . . .

Cash Compensation: How much do you get and when will you get it? Is it based on hitting certain milestones or on hours spent on the business? Will compensation be in the form of salary or distributions? Do you have to take cash, or could you exchange it for more shares instead?

. . . .

Expenses: What's your policy on expenses? How much entertaining can you do? Who writes the reimbursement checks?

(continued on next page)

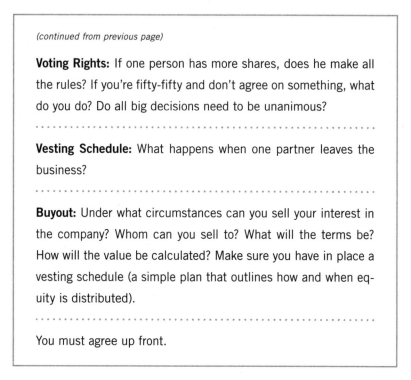

(continued from previous page)

Voting Rights: If one person has more shares, does he make all the rules? If you're fifty-fifty and don't agree on something, what do you do? Do all big decisions need to be unanimous?

. . . .

Vesting Schedule: What happens when one partner leaves the business?

. . . .

Buyout: Under what circumstances can you sell your interest in the company? Whom can you sell to? What will the terms be? How will the value be calculated? Make sure you have in place a vesting schedule (a simple plan that outlines how and when equity is distributed).

. . . .

You must agree up front.

This Is What You Asked For!

Your company wants to build something. You want to go to market fast. Having managed to scrape together enough money to add a couple full-time employees to your team, you need to launch before your competition catches up. Due to your finite budget and time constraints, the realization dawns: You need to outsource.

Today outsourcing is often a critical part of launching a new business or product, but it's an area where many people fall down.

A few years ago I had started to launch an online marketplace in the health-care industry that would provide seniors with better prices and easier access to a variety of services. I tried hard to assemble a team of developers. I wanted to get something up quickly and test the market response. All the best people I contacted were busy on other projects, so I reached out to a few friends, asking what they would do. One told me that to solve a similar problem, he'd hired a firm in India to build his company's Web site.

I decided to do the same. I contacted the outfit my friend had used and we had a one-hour call to get acquainted. I shared my idea over the phone, and they responded with an overview of how they would execute my vision. We negotiated a price and signed an agreement. I was in business.

A month later I got an e-mail with a link to my new Web site. It was a disaster! The graphic design, the look and feel, the user experience, and the functionality were all wrong. To make matters worse, I had planned to use the site for an investor presentation later that week. Now I would have nothing to show. I was extremely frustrated. I just didn't understand why there was such a big disconnect.

In outsourcing, I had set aside everything I knew about hiring and running a project. I had given the consultants a general project description, expecting them to fill in the blanks when I hadn't really thought through everything myself. I had put my entire business in their hands instead of just giving them one product or feature as a test. I hadn't checked in along the way, so the first thing I had seen was their finished product. As a result, I had had no idea they were on the wrong track. Because I had been so vague with regard to what I wanted, they had been forced to make decisions for me. While some were good, most went against my vision for the product.

When I told them how upset I was and asked them to explain themselves, they said, "This is *exactly* what you asked for!" And frankly, they were right.

How do you avoid some of the common pitfalls in outsourcing?

Be disciplined. It doesn't matter if your consultant is an overseas developer or someone right across the street. The same rules apply as far as clearly communicating your expectations.

Hire right. Do not take anyone's word for work quality. Operate with the same amount of diligence you would when making full-time hires. Check references to get a better picture of past performance. Agree upon a very clear job description and, if possible, run a test by executing a small project together before handing over too much responsibility. If you're not getting what you want, don't waste time. Cut your losses and move on.

Even if a consultant is recommended by valued friends, use caution. I've found that most people are not very careful when referring consultants, who may be between gigs, out of work, or juggling lots of projects. Some are friends of the people making the referral and the favor is being done for them, not you. Or the referrer knows them socially rather than from a business relationship.

Provide very clear direction. If you paint an incomplete picture of your intended outcome, you'll get something that only vaguely resembles what you had in mind.

Many entrepreneurs have a vision with no concrete idea of how to execute, so they hand the job over to someone else, expecting that person to magically fill in the blanks. With a full-time employee, that may work. Your staff can plug in details; that's one of the things you hired them to do. And since they are right there in the office, you can exercise some direct control. This gives your team the benefit of receiving feedback every single day.

Consultants, on the other hand, are typically not in the office, so they are not as in sync with the day-to-day business. As a result, they can't fill in certain gaps in the direction they are given. Therefore, in most cases they do only what they are told. That's usually a good thing, because if they start getting creative, they could take the project in the wrong direction. Therefore, you have to work twice as hard with consultants to make sure you provide excellent direction, management, and oversight. I always recommend that a company have its best manager oversee all consultants during the launch period.

Use examples. When dealing with consultants, it may be helpful to find examples of other products, services, features, etc. that you want to use as models in order to translate your vision into something tangible that others can easily grasp.

For example, if you are developing an e-commerce site, what is the specific desired user experience? What are the steps in the buying process? How do you picture that in your mind? The clearer you can be, the more likely you are to get the result you want. Point consultants to two or three comparable Web sites you like that they can use as models or guides when building yours.

Check in regularly. Create a regular schedule for checking in with your consultant and providing feedback. The more often you provide feedback, the happier you will be with the end product.

Manage against clear deliverables. It is important to specify key milestones and delivery dates. That keeps both sides honest and up-to-date, helping to ensure the contractor is making progress.

Pay based on performance. Sometimes the supplier will want everything up front or payment at regular intervals, but a better approach is to pay based on performance. What you see is what you pay for.

Take responsibility. If your first reaction on seeing your product is, *Hey, this isn't what I intended,* that's not the end of the world—and another reason why we only build one thing at a time. Don't take your disappointment out on your contractor: How much of the fault was yours for not being clear or for not checking in? You may decide after seeing a prototype that in fact you want something different altogether. Instead of losing your temper, outline what you like and what you would like to improve. Communicate this feedback in a constructive way.

Although the inspiration, the initial hard work, and the passion for your Big Idea may rest solely with you, the entrepreneur, you cannot overestimate the importance of having the right team in place. Spending time and energy on hiring the right people (and quickly letting go of the ones who don't work out) can truly make the difference between a business that launches successfully in ninety days and one that never gets off the ground.

CHAPTER 6.

UNLOCKING CREATIVITY

The problem is not the problem. The problem is your attitude
about the problem.
—CAPTAIN JACK SPARROW, *PIRATES OF THE CARIBBEAN*

Torn Carpet, Chipped Paint

In the middle of the dot-com boom, the market was hot. Companies were springing out of the ground almost overnight, and I was getting calls every day to help them launch.

In 1998 I decided to test the job market and had a series of interviews in Silicon Valley. I remember walking into beautiful lobbies with expensive furniture. People were moving around the office on scooters, and one company even had a slide in the middle of its workspace. All these companies were trying to sell their cool cultures.

I was about to take a job offer when a good friend from my days at Quote.com, Russell Hyzen, gave me a call. He had gone off to become the first employee at Xoom.com, an online community and e-commerce business. It was looking to fill a role, and he knew I was in the market.

When I arrived for my interview, I found that Xoom's offices were in a beautiful landmark building off California Street in downtown San Francisco. But inside? I almost fell over when I saw the torn green carpet and the chipped paint falling off the walls.

There was no receptionist. Instead, Chris Kitze, the company's founder and CEO, had an office near the front door. He was the first person to greet people as they walked in.

I soon learned that Chris had a vision, one that became a shared vision of everyone he brought into the company. He hired the best people, gave them access to the resources they needed—and then got out of their way. He was absolutely committed to seeing everyone on the team win: If the company made money, they would too.

When I talked to the team, there was a pride of ownership that I hadn't seen anywhere else, and a common purpose and community that wasn't present in the fancier offices. I could see why many of the people I met at Xoom had followed Chris from one company to another.

The company had money, so I had to ask: *Why the torn carpet and the chipped paint?* "That's not important," Chris said. As an owner, he believed the best use of funds was to invest the money back into the company, into hiring the best people, into building a great business. If he did that, the rest would take care of itself.

Unlikely as it may seem, that torn carpet and chipped paint became a symbol of pride everyone shared within the organization. It is part of what got me to join the company, and our team built a great business, took it public, and eventually merged with NBC to create NBC Internet.

The culture didn't stop at pride of ownership. It was also sales driven. Everyone knew our number one goal was to generate revenues. We knew that without cash coming in the door, we had no business. Chris set the tone, signing all his e-mails with the tagline "Go Sell Something." Every day, in every e-mail, those words reinforced the focus, and not just with salespeople. Everybody in the company came to think of himself or herself as a salesperson, which meant he or she approached problems and the product in a way that was very customer-centric.

Soon after I arrived, I saw how valuable the sales-driven culture could be. Times got tough in the second half of 1998. I returned from a vacation to find the stock market going sideways. As a result, we lost the investment bank that we had thought would take us public. We were nearly out of cash, but Chris's culture saved us. Even though many of the most talented people could easily have found great jobs at other companies in those days of the Internet boom, nobody jumped ship. We had a sense of community and knew we could sell our way out of any problem by generating the cash we needed to get through it.

What are the key factors in creating a great culture for your new business?

Establish a clear vision. That way everyone runs in the same direction. How do you create a clear vision? Ask yourself this question: *Where do we want to go?*

The answer should be a clear description of what you would like to achieve over a specific period of time. This creates a framework for the company and serves as a guide for choosing current and future courses of action.

A vision statement is different from a mission statement. A vision statement answers the question "Where do we want to go?" A mission statement answers the question "Why do we exist?" A vision statement is shared within the company. The mission statement is shared with the outside world.

Hire great people and give them access to resources. Invest money in great people. Give them access to all the resources they need. Help them solve problems and remove roadblocks so they can do their jobs. Then get out of their way.

Be absolutely committed to seeing everyone on the team win. From the top down, everyone must be committed to seeing the team as a whole win. As an entrepreneur (and the person taking on most of the risk), you are certainly entitled to earn more in the long run than anyone else. But shared ownership, structured in the right way, in which everyone knows their role and the impact they are having on results, creates a culture that can't be beat.

That may sound like a simple recipe, but too many companies fall short of it, and as a result they don't succeed at the level they should. And this isn't about getting one of these things right. As a leader you need to be committed to all of them. If you are, you will significantly increase your chance of success.

Vegas and Video Games

Building a culture of teamwork is only one part of the equation. You also need to build a culture of innovation. How do you inspire people to open their minds in a way that unlocks creativity within your organization and achieves the best results? Let me share a story about how a former colleague named Ed attained legendary status for his ability to unlock creativity (*and* have a great time in the process).

Ed's goal was to change the way that products were marketed in his client's business. He saw that everyone in the industry had been speaking to customers in the same old way for years. So he decided to turn things on their head. He needed to unlock his team's creativity, and to do so he made a pretty radical move: He took the whole creative and account team to Las Vegas.

He told them almost nothing about what he had planned for the trip.

On day one the team arrived and partied, going to the best restaurants and clubs and doing some gambling. Some of the crew stayed up all night. No work got done.

On day two Ed told his people there was nothing on the agenda other than having more fun. So they did more of the same: eating, drinking, gambling, clubbing.

Day three? Still no agenda. Nothing. So they went at it again: best restaurants, best clubs, a nonstop party.

On morning number four, Ed's tone changed. Over the past few days, he had helped his team leave their lives, stresses, and responsibilities behind. Now he wanted something from them. He gathered the group and told them, "We have a mission. Our mission is to revolutionize the way products are marketed and sold in our industry. We need to be creative, different, and unique. We need to appeal to our client's core young male audience—and they play lots of video games."

While Ed was speaking, video-game systems were being installed in each team member's room. For the next two days, he instructed, they were not to leave their hotel rooms: Their job had become to play video games. That was it! They were supposed to think about the whole experience of playing a game, including the graphics, the sounds, and the characters that appealed to the target audience. He wanted them to consider how game designers presented content, how they manipulated the look and feel of the product for the customer. He asked them to pay attention to the scoreboards, the sound effects, and every other little trick the gamers had devised. Most of all, he wanted his team to think about how his client could build upon video-game innovations to make its real-life products win a new generation of customers.

After three glorious days in the sun, his team wasted no time in unleashing their creativity and creating a variety of innovations that turned their client's industry upside down!

Could Ed's team have accomplished the same results playing games back in their offices in Los Angeles? I doubt it. By taking his team to Las Vegas, he shifted them from *work* mode to *play* mode. He put people together who normally did not have much time to interact in a fun, social setting. The days of partying in Las Vegas brought them closer, building camaraderie and a sense of teamwork. Two guys in a hotel room playing a video game see their jobs differently from how they would seated in adjacent cubicles, looking at their computers.

Now I'm not saying you need to take your team to Vegas (or anywhere else) for a week. But to foster creative teamwork, you need to find a way to get them out of the office mind-set and open their minds. You need to tap the genius within each of them and do so on a regular basis. Being creative applies to all aspects of your business, from building something cool to breaking down barriers when trying to sell your product.

Part of Ed's legacy is that creativity has become an essential part of the culture at his company. They are still thinking outside the box, still building great products. You can too, with the following recommendations.

Bring groups together. When you are launching a new business or product, team members are busy. All of them have their heads down, focused on what they are responsible for. Most of their time is spent working with other people in their department, meaning business, creative, and technical people don't get much time to interact. There are ways to change that.

At Xoom we had pizza and beer at three o'clock every Friday afternoon. People from different groups got to meet and interact in a social environment. As the company grew, those Friday afternoons offered an opportunity to meet new team members, and together we evolved a shared vision of the company. Even if people with different responsibilities looked at the company in different ways, over beer and pizza we came up with some of our best and most creative—and collaborative—ideas.

Encourage risk. You win some, you lose some. But people always need to be encouraged to take risk. They need to know that even if something does not work, if risk has been mitigated the experience is a valuable part of growing a business. The best way to do this is to make lots of small bets. That way, if something does not work, there is no threat or concern that it will put the entire operation or the person's job at risk.

Get out regularly. Do something outside the office at least once a quarter. The activity doesn't have to be expensive or extravagant. You might schedule a happy hour, miniature golf, or go-cart racing. Whatever it is, getting people to engage in a new setting can build relationships and inspire creativity.

Once you've developed a sound business plan, put the right people in place to execute, and created a culture that encourages openness, innovation, and risk taking, you will have built a great foundation for the business to succeed. You will also be in a position to move to the next step in the process: raising capital.

OPENING MINDS

Combine Business with Pleasure: Take your workers out to play— to the ballpark, to karaoke, for a brainstorming session over beers. Bring pizza into the office on Friday afternoons. Do something different on a regular basis. Getting your employees out of their comfort zones and interacting with one another can open their eyes to new possibilities.

(continued on next page)

(continued from previous page)

Encourage Experimentation: Declare that for a few hours every month no one is allowed to use their computer or their smart phone. In place of screens, issue every employee a notebook and ask them to spend the time writing, sketching, and diagramming their thoughts and ideas on how to improve the business and innovate. The shock of putting pen to paper will force them to think in a different way. After the exercise, encourage them to tear pages out of their notebooks and post them on a brainstorming wall.

Make Small Bets: Encourage your team to experiment with side projects. Many of these will fail, but one of them may turn into your next big idea.

If Something Doesn't Work, Celebrate the Fact That Your Team Took a Shot: People who are the most successful and creative are the ones who take risks. They tried, they failed, and they learned from their mistakes. Create a culture where taking a shot at something new is celebrated, as long as something is learned.

CHAPTER 7.

RAISING CAPITAL

And where I excel is ridiculous, sickening, work ethic. You know, while the other guy's sleeping? I'm working.

—WILL SMITH

Trading for Tickets

Most entrepreneurs start businesses from the same place: *nowhere.* Despite beginning with little or nothing, the best of them bootstrap, and through their own sheer will, hard work, and effort they find ways to make things happen. They manage to be resourceful and pull together what their business needs to launch.

As an entrepreneur you have to figure out ways to keep pushing your business forward, largely by yourself. You have to take whatever you have that is of value and leverage, trade, share, or swap it. That often means that founders of bootstrapping start-ups forgo paychecks, offer their services as consultants, give away early products and services for nothing, and do lots of moonlighting, at least until the new venture generates enough cash to survive on its own.

Intrapreneurs also self-fund, by adding the new project to their existing responsibilities. They effectively take on twice as much work with no additional pay to help get their idea off the ground. They have to become masters of juggling not only their core business but also their new-project responsibilities. Since management does not want to see either one struggle, intrapreneurs take on not only reputation risk but also job-security risk. Only once the new project hits certain milestones may the intrapreneur be able to get more resources for the new project and a bigger paycheck.

Bootstrapping is more vital today than ever. Many investors are reluctant to put money into a venture until it is already generating positive cash flow. Compared with the days before the global economic crash of 2008, investors now have far less appetite for risk, meaning most won't reach into their pockets until you've taken your business beyond the early stages and proven your model. As a result, new business owners have to bootstrap longer than they did in the past.

My first exposure to bootstrapping came compliments of Tony Robbins. I wasn't raising money for a new business, but it sure taught me how to be scrappy. I was twenty-one years old, and my title was "field sales representative and national sales trainer." As an advance man responsible for filling the seats in Robbins's seminars, I would travel with a handful of my peers to a city where Tony was to speak, and we would promote his event. The primary program I sold was called "Power to Influence," and it focused on sales and persuasion.

Before our team went into the field, we immersed ourselves in the content. We had to be passionate about Tony's message, because our task was to drum up interest and sell tickets for his programs. We spoke to small groups, sometimes five times a day, seven days a week. We'd share a few program highlights, talk about what people would gain by attending, and try to sell as many tickets as we could in order to make big sales commissions.

In retrospect I realize that this experience not only taught me about sales and persuasion but also gave me a bunch of survival skills that would later come in handy when I became an entrepreneur.

I spent two to three months at a time in cities like Detroit, Toronto, Vancouver, Boston, Houston, Seattle, and Los Angeles. No one on the team collected a salary and we didn't have expense accounts. We paid for our own rental cars. Nobody even had a phone! Basically, we were given a plane ticket, a place to stay, and a couple of initial bookings. After that we had to live off the land.

We did, however, have something valuable in our pockets: Our currency was tickets to Robbins's events. We learned how to barter tickets and our own speaking and coaching in return for what we needed. This was a key moment in my business education, a sort of Bootstrapping 101.

Here's how it worked. When we got off the plane in a new city, we would decide who was going out in search of what. The first priority was always to get cars and cell phones. We would split up and go to car dealerships, where we would talk general managers into giving us cars for a couple of months. In exchange we'd provide in-house training and give their entire sales teams tickets to one of Tony's events. Same thing at cell-phone stores and gyms. One guy even bartered for time at a tanning salon.

Like a pack of lions hunting, we had to work together as a team. We learned that as long as you have both persistence and a deep supply of something with perceived value (in our case, Tony Robbins tickets), you can catch all the antelope (or cars and phones) you need to survive.

That same scrappiness applies to bootstrapping your own business. You have to be creative, mastering the art of trading with others. It's about offering value for value.

Here are a few questions to get you started:

Where do you need help? What do you need that you can't afford to go out and buy? Do you need a Web site, design, marketing, social-media, accounting, or legal advice? What will each of these things cost?

What's your currency? What do you have of value to offer? Can you provide consulting help with others' businesses, introduce them to key prospects, or provide a service that they need?

Who are your trading partners? Take a close look at your network and identify other entrepreneurs you can barter and partner with. What you will find is a trading economy in today's market you probably did not know existed. And don't be afraid to go to prospective customers. You might be surprised how often they will be willing to give you access to certain resources in exchange for being first in line when your new product or service is ready.

Where's the cheap labor? Even if you can't afford to pay big salaries yet, there are many people out there who will work for free in exchange for a promise of future compensation. These could include people out of work, in transition, or trying to find something part time. The opportunity to get in on the ground floor of something they believe in may be enough to get them started.

Create a list of people you know who have what you need. Prioritize the list, placing the services you need most at the top. Find out which people in your network offer those services *and* need the most help with their own businesses. Then see if there is a way to trade, borrow, or swap services in a way that helps both parties move their businesses forward.

Cannibal Women in the Avocado Jungle of Death

Like it or not, a new business sometimes requires a capital investment beyond the bounds of bootstrapping. Unfortunately, money, as the saying goes, doesn't grow on trees (even if, in reading about some start-ups, it seems like people can't give it away fast enough).

The hard facts are that less than a third of all businesses ever take any outside capital, and of the ones that do, most have typically been in business for three years or more. Making your pitch to a series of potential money sources can feel like a distraction while you're trying to run a business. It will involve working your network, setting up meetings, putting together materials, following up, and closing the sale.

Raising capital takes persistence, whether you are an entrepreneur pitching to individual investors or an intrapreneur working to build consensus for funding within a big organization. Most investors probably won't agree to put money into your company, but that doesn't mean you stop looking. Go into each meeting with the objective of listening to all the feedback the investors have to offer and applying what you learn going forward. For example, your investors may have excellent ideas on how to improve your pitch, find additional revenue, reduce your start-up costs, separate yourself from the competition, and find strategic partners. By listening and following good advice, you're bringing yourself one step closer to finding the finances you need.

I've always been inspired by my friend Gary Goldstein, whose story is a classic tale of persistence. Gary started out as a criminal-defense attorney, but his real passion was storytelling. So he decided to move to Hollywood and launch a career in the entertainment business. There he managed young writers and directors before making the decision to produce films. Gary went on to produce some of the top box-office hits of all time, including *Pretty Woman*, the highest-grossing live-action film in Disney's history and a beloved classic.

When Gary decided to produce his first film, he didn't have all the money and resources he needed. He teamed with an up-and-coming writer. The two bootstrapped as long as they could. Then it was time to go and raise outside capital to get his film, a comedy-horror thriller, made. That part certainly wasn't easy, but Gary never thought about quitting. Making a film was his passion and, as he told me, "you have to chase your passion like it's the last bus of the night." Through Gary's persistence and pigheaded determination, he raised two hundred thousand dollars to make the film. It was titled *Cannibal Women in the Avocado Jungle of Death*.

In addition to having a tight budget, a scheduling conflict left Gary and his partner with only four weeks from the day they closed their financing to cast, film, edit, and deliver the final product. That may sound impossible to us, but it wasn't to Gary. He was committed to making this project a success. He did not believe in waiting for the "perfect time" or "perfect circumstances" to get started. Instead he believed that being in the game was better than waiting around on the sidelines. With that mentality, he devised a plan to spend two weeks preparing the project and two weeks for everything else.

But at the end of the first week, Gary was up against a real problem. The film had no cast and crew; it was just Gary and his writer. Instead of shutting down, Gary persevered, because he believed that "success is far more likely when you choose persistence over doubt and inaction."

Gary and his writer hit the phones, called all their friends, asked them to call their friends, and invited them out to the set. They decided if someone showed up who dressed well, that person would be in charge of wardrobe. If someone had a camera, he or she would be the cinematographer. Casting consisted of seeing who arrived on the set each day. This was guerrilla filmmaking at its best. Somehow that film, which ended up starring Shannon Tweed and Bill Maher, came together. It ran on cable for the next fifteen years and became a cult classic. The experience was successful enough that Gary was able to dissolve his management firm and become a full-time independent producer.

I asked Gary what he learned most from that experience. "You don't have to be a master at something to achieve something worthwhile," he said. "Just by sheer will and stubbornness you can accomplish anything you set out to do."

The True Path to Raising Capital

Starting a business, raising money, and executing your Big Idea is not easy, but people do it successfully every day.

When it comes to raising capital, the challenges most entrepreneurs face are inexperience and overly optimistic expectations with regard to how much time and effort raising capital really takes. Many spend their time talking to the wrong people about their investment, and when the opportunity hits them, they are not armed with the tools they need to successfully close the deal.

If you combine these strategies for raising capital with the lesson of Gary's persistence and determination, you will be successful. But before we get started, keep these considerations in mind.

Raising capital takes time. Many people think that investors will jump on their Big Idea right away and that they won't be out there raising money for long. From the time you make your first fund-raising call, figure on six months to a year to close a big round of financing. If you would like to speed that process up to, say, ninety days, place your focus on raising a very small amount of capital with the purpose of building and testing a basic product and taking it to market. It is much easier for investors to make small bets and put less money at risk. Creating proof of concept for a basic version of your idea in such a short period of time also makes it much more likely that you can bring these investors back for more capital—and at a higher valuation.

Raising capital takes hard work. This process alone can seem like a full-time job, but you need to get in front of a lot of people. I estimate that for every twenty-five to thirty qualified investors you pitch, you will close one.

Raising capital can be very stressful. Your potential investors are busy. They can be tough to get on the calendar. They miss meetings. They go on vacation. You often won't get the answer you expect. You may not like what they tell you about your project. Managing your emotions and staying focused despite delays and setbacks is essential. Keep asking yourself, *What can I take away from that meeting or prospect that can be applied to my business or fund-raising? How do I use those lessons as fuel to close my next prospect?*

Keep your business moving forward. Raising capital takes time, but that's no excuse to stop executing your plan. You will need to bootstrap, be resourceful, and look for every opportunity to continue building while raising capital, balancing both objectives. Continuing to build will pay off, as you'll find that even small, incremental steps make a huge difference in terms of getting investors. The more of your idea they can see coming to life, the easier it is for them to get their arms around you, your team, and your product. The further along you are, the less risk is involved for an investor, meaning you will get better financing terms on your deal. Staying at it pays off. Be like Gary: If you knock on enough of the right doors, with the right story and materials in place, you will eventually get your shot.

Don't settle for "no." I have amazing kids and I think they would be great at raising money. Why? Because kids just won't take no for an answer. They keep coming back. They face rejection. It doesn't bother them. Instead, they learn from it. They take note of what didn't work. Then they come right back and try another way to get what they are after. Don't be afraid to be a kid again!

Where Will the Money Come From?

So where is all this money going to come from? Who's going to invest in you? There are several options when launching a new business or product. To help save time and get you to market faster, here is a list of capital resources. To get started, put most of your energy into the source that is the best fit with your personal network, business goals, and stage of investment.

Friends and family. If you are an entrepreneur launching a new business or taking a new product to market, those closest to you are usually the very first capital providers you should consider. Your friends, family, or company may make funds available even when your new venture is still in the idea phase while other professionally managed sources of capital may not be options before there's a product or prototype to validate the idea. Most friend or family investments range from $1,000 to $25,000, and they may be in the form of equity (ownership in the company) or debt (a simple loan).

Angel investors. Angels are wealthy individuals, often entrepreneurs just like you, who are willing to invest anywhere from $25,000 to $250,000. Angels typically work as individuals or through clubs with other angel investors, putting money into start-ups and early-stage businesses. Apart from monetary investment, they may be looking to be involved and can be great coaches for the enterprises in which they invest. Their investment is typically in industries with which they are familiar and can be equity or debt.

Crowdfunding. This source makes use of online and off-line networks to attract informal (and sometimes professional) investors to buy into an idea or company. The concept of crowdfunding is to generate investments from the masses, to get small amounts of money from a large number of individuals. There are many forms of crowdfunding, including donation-based, equity-based, revenue-sharing, and peer-to-peer lending.

Venture capital. Venture capital is almost always provided in exchange for equity in your company. VCs are very sophisticated investors. Although they have a financial focus, many can also provide significant managerial, operational, and technical expertise. In return they look for a bigger portion of equity and sometimes even a controlling interest (meaning they assume more than half of the equity and/or decision-making power in your company). Investments from venture capital typically begin around $250,000 and can go up to millions of dollars.

OTHER OPTIONS FOR FINANCING YOUR BUSINESS

Business Incubators: Incubators are programs designed to support the growth of early-stage entrepreneurial efforts. Often they will invest between $5,000 and $25,000. They will work very closely with the company to help get the business in the best shape possible to raise more capital and go to market. Incubators are typically industry specific (for example, technology or energy), and their partners bring significant industry experience, resources, and contacts.

Business Accelerators: Accelerators are similar, but they tend to focus on companies that have gone to market and are beginning a growth phase. Many business accelerators are backed by venture capitalists who want to get a foothold in what they believe to be a good emerging business.

The Big Meeting

If you've hung out with founders as much as I have, you've inevitably heard the following line: "I have a big meeting with an investor coming up." Because the entrepreneur got the appointment, he's certain the investor has real interest. The entrepreneur's growing enthusiasm leads him to think the money is in the bag—only to come back from the big meeting empty-handed and deeply disappointed at the result.

For the typical entrepreneur, raising money is an entirely foreign experience. The challenge is, investors often have been doing their jobs for years. Your inexperience puts you at an immediate disadvantage. We need to get you up to speed quickly; with just ninety days, there is no time to waste. The place to start is making sure you get yourself in front of the right people. The process starts with doing your homework.

Investors have a mandate to make money, and typically they have a specific formula to mitigate their risk. That makes it imperative that you understand their focus. Some things for you to consider include:

Background. What companies have your potential investors worked for? What's their functional expertise? Often they will invest only in what they know. As an example, if they spent their career in real estate, they will have a deep understanding of how to analyze the true value of a real-estate deal, how to get involved in ways that help the entrepreneur, and how to step in and help turn the ship if things go sideways. Because of all this, they'll be more likely to invest.

Previous investments. Know the kinds of companies they have invested in in the past (the typical real-estate investor probably won't invest in, say, software). If you pitch someone in a consumer Internet business and he or she invests only in energy, it won't matter how good your idea is—he or she will pass. Be aware, as well, that if you are dealing with a venture-capital or professional-investment firm, you could be in the right place but talking to the wrong person. Find out which investor inside fits your deal best.

Stage of investment. Does your potential investor favor seed or early-stage companies, have minimum revenue criteria, or have other key requirements before stepping into a deal? If you present your business at a stage other than your investor's sweet spot, he or she probably won't be interested. That is true of both individuals and large firms. Keep in mind that many professional investors raise money from other investors with a mandate to invest in a specific type and stage of company.

Size of investment. Ten thousand dollars? A hundred thousand? A million? Be clear that what you're asking for is in line with what they put into individual investments.

Expected return. Are they looking to get double, five times, ten times what they invest?

Investment horizon. When do they expect a return on their capital? What time period do they have in mind—to get in and out within a year, three years, or five? Everyone needs to have the same expectations on day one.

How do you find these things out? Do your homework. If you can't find an answer to a specific question, just ask. Asking good questions will help you establish yourself as professional and someone who respects a potential investor's time, which earns you bonus points too.

Knowing these things in advance will help you operate with speed and efficiency, saving you valuable time and money. It will help ensure that every meeting is with a qualified investor. That way your "big meeting" will be exactly what you expect.

One last thing: *believe.*

Raising money is no small task. No matter how good you and your product are, it is a time-consuming and labor-intensive process. But when you've done your homework and go into meetings with the right people, you will know that, on some level, they really want to invest in you. Their mandate is to find companies just like yours. They are hoping that you are the person who can deliver what they want. In fact, they probably want this meeting as much, if not more, than you do!

So do your homework, get in front of the right people—and execute once you are there.

LOANS VERSUS CONVERTIBLE EQUITY

What's the difference?

. . . .

Loans: Loans are simply an amount of money lent by one person or entity to another person or entity. In general, there is an interest payment (an annual percentage of the original loan amount). Things to consider include guaranteed or nonguaranteed, simple or compound interest, and the amount of time given to repay the principal.

(continued on next page)

(continued from previous page)

Equity: Equity is an ownership interest in a business. Equity holders negotiate a variety of terms associated with certain rights and controls.

. . . .

Convertible Notes: These are similar to loans except that, at the end of the loan period, the investors can opt either to have their principal returned (as with a standard loan arrangement) *or* to convert that investment into equity in the business. Convertible notes have been very popular for early-stage companies in the last few years because they are a low-cost means of closing financial deals (the legal costs are substantially less than with other options). In addition, investors sometimes favor them because they typically earn high interest during the start-up phase while retaining the option to leave if the business doesn't perform as expected.

The Fastest Way to the Door

Having spent years both in businesses at all stages of raising capital and investing in other people's companies, I've been on both sides of the table. As a result, I've learned firsthand what to do—and what not to do—when presenting to an investor. I've also learned there are certain mistakes you can make that will kill a potential investor's interest and lead you right out the door.

We only have ninety days to go from idea to market, so avoid the mistakes below in order to keep the process moving forward and ultimately get the results you want.

Appropriate domain and stage expertise. Investors fund people, not ideas. They want founders and management who have deep domain experience. In the early stages they like a background that includes running fast-paced, resource-constrained environments and thus might see it as a risk if, for example, someone from a *Fortune 500* company were seeking to launch a start-up or a technology pro shifted into real estate.

"We are first to market." As an entrepreneur you may think this is a big advantage, but such a claim can actually work against you. Typically, being first to market means you take on all the risk. You'll spend lots of your time educating people, and to an investor that says *expensive*. Many would rather be second, riding in the wake of the first company.

"We have no competition." Making this claim may be the most common mistake of entrepreneurs raising capital. On hearing it, the experienced investor will assume one of three things: that you are lying, that you do not really know your market, or that there have been others before you who did not make it. As soon as you speak those words, your proposal is most likely headed into the trash.

"We need a million dollars to get started." Why? Investors will do everything they can to minimize their risk every step of the way. They will want to know if there's another way, whether you can start with something smaller and more focused. Can you get to market faster and get enough feedback to get a sense that you're heading in the right direction *before* investing that million dollars into a product no one may want?

"If I build it, they will come." Maybe that works in movies, but I've never seen it work anywhere else—and neither has your investor. It takes time, effort, and money to build a customer base.

"We have more features than anyone else." Who cares? That does not mean your target customer will like all of them. An investor would rather know that you have one functioning feature that your target customer likes than that you have ten untested ones.

"The big companies are too big or slow to compete." Not if they are serious, they aren't. If a market is big enough, there is a good chance someone in the industry is taking a look. If they decide there is an opportunity, they certainly have the resources in place to jump into your market and have an impact. This does not mean they will be successful, but they could be disruptive. If big companies have not entered, they may think the market is too small.

"We do lots of things well." I always ask entrepreneurs what *one thing* their business is really great at, the one thing that separates it from everyone else. Most of the time they do not know. Instead they rattle off three or four things they think the company does equally well. Telling an investor that you are great at everything communicates that you don't really understand what business you are in.

"We do that too." If, during a meeting, an investor suggests additional products or services that might be a good fit or points to things the competition is doing, don't respond to each comment by saying, "Oh, we do that too." Many entrepreneurs think they need to demonstrate that they are "on top of everything," building "every bell and whistle" in the marketplace. But this sort of response communicates a lack of focus. Instead, acknowledge that the investor's suggestions may be great to add down the road but make it clear that for now you're focused on this one thing.

Don't be afraid to say, "I don't know." Some entrepreneurs think they need to be expert at everything. As a result, they try to answer every question that comes their way, even if they have no clue what they are talking about. If you talk in circles, that'll be obvious to the investor. Since everyone knows that a new business or product is surrounded by uncertainty, people understand that assumptions need to be made and lessons need to be learned. One of the signs of strength investors look for in an entrepreneur is the simple understanding that no one has all the answers. Letting investors see that quality in you communicates that they can trust you to be straightforward and open to collaboration.

"Writing a business plan would just slow us down." Investors know that without a plan you have not forced yourself to test your model, that you have no real sense of income and expenses or of capital requirements and timing. That also conveys that everyone isn't on the same page. How could they be without a written plan to provide them with a singular focus that keeps the team grounded?

OTHER RED FLAGS

A few additional factors that could affect an investor's decision regarding your business include:

. . . .

High Failure Rate: Some industries have significantly higher failure rates than others (restaurants and retail stores are good examples). That certainly does not mean you will not succeed, but you'll need to have a very clear plan.

. . . .

Dependence on Legal or Government Regulation: Industries that tend to be more litigious than others or subject to much legal regulation may make investors hesitate. If your product requires long government approvals or a bidding process, there could be additional cause for concern because of the potential drain on cash. Investment in such businesses is not for everyone.

(continued on next page)

(continued from previous page)

Key Operations in Different Places: If your company is based in one place (e.g., a certain country or geographic region) and key operations are elsewhere, that can be a cause for concern. Separation can create an added level of complexity when managing a fast-moving business.

. . . .

Small Returns for Investors: Your potential investors may believe in the product and the market, even that you have the right team to execute, that everything is in place. But your business still may not meet their investment criteria, with anticipated returns that are too low; or they may view it as a lifestyle business and think you will want to stay with it forever, leaving them with no chance at a big exit. Chances are, though, what you're offering will be perfect for someone else. Keep trying.

The Callback

In the entertainment business you audition. Your goal is to get invited to the next step, so you wait for the callback. The same is true in raising capital. With each interaction you try to generate enough interest and momentum to move to the next step.

Here are a few tips to get investors to make that call, to summon you back.

Build a great team. People invest in teams, so make sure you build a great one, from partners to employees, from consultants to collaborators. Make it your mission to surround yourself with the best. Avoid being strong in just one area. Cross-functional expertise that sees business in different ways adds perspective and gives your investors confidence.

Feed information in bite-size chunks. This is a rule of thumb in direct-response marketing. For example, the purpose of the headline is to get you to read the first line. The purpose of the first line is to get you to read the second line; and so on. Eventually you build momentum and you close a sale. That's your goal.

Don't send investors everything at once. If you overburden them, they'll walk away feeling overwhelmed and confused. Instead, feed them small, digestible pieces. For example, start by sending your target a one-paragraph overview of the business via e-mail. If there is interest, send a one-page executive summary. If he is still keen, follow up with a short PowerPoint presentation. Every communication should build on the one before.

Tailor each communication to your audience. Each investor will ask a different set of questions and have a different set of concerns after each communication. Your job is to get all of these questions and concerns on the table, then apply what you've learned in tailoring your next communication. Let's say one investor has concerns about the market. At the next step, build a short presentation that specifically addresses that investor's anxieties; your next conversation should cover just that, nothing else. Once you get past that issue, move on to the next.

Another reason not to send everything at once is that the materials need to be tailored for each investor target. Information prepared for one person may not be right for another person, and you can shoot yourself in the foot. Take a cautious, step-by-step approach to learning, iterating, and then improving your presentations in order to suit each and every conversation.

Be open to feedback and ask for advice. Don't take anything personally. Use every piece of feedback you get, no matter how positive or negative, as fuel to power you forward. No matter how much you don't want to hear it or how much your point of view may be in direct contrast, approach everything with an openness to learn. That openness and flexibility are great signs of leadership in early-stage environments.

Tricks of the Trade

Capital raising means you must not only focus on getting money but also, in doing so, seek the most favorable terms, trade the least possible equity, and maintain control of the business.

In shaping your thinking, consider these factors:

How much money do you really need? My advice is to raise just what you think you'll need, then a little bit more. By running lean, your team stays focused, and you'll make better decisions and avoid waste.

Early-stage investors will want a big piece of your company. They probably deserve it for assuming the risk of investing in a business or product that still has a long way to go (they've seen the statistics about how many start-ups fail). They expect to build that risk into what they charge for their capital, demanding more equity, higher interest rates, more control, or other terms. That also means that the more money you raise up front, the more of your company you will have to give away in the form of equity.

Be thrifty. Take in as little money as you can and give away as little of your company as possible. Prove your concept sooner, then go out and raise more money when your company has earned a higher valuation.

Loans. Loans can be guaranteed or nonguaranteed. Will the interest be simple or compound? How much time do you have to repay the principal?

Equity. How much equity will you give away? Will your investor(s) be active or passive? How much control will you relinquish? Do your money sources wish to be involved in big decisions or plan to leave them to you and the team? What kind of return are they expecting? When do they plan to see this return?

Entrepreneurs are optimists; they tend to focus on their current round of financing and often significantly underestimate their long-term capital requirements. As a result, they part with a lot of their company's equity early, thinking they will not need to give much away down the road. They spread it around to investors, employees, contractors, and advisers. Later, when they go out to raise additional capital, they may find that a new round will cause them to become minority shareholders or lose control of their business. Keep in mind that it's common to seek capital more than once in a company's lifetime.

The decisions you make early will have a lasting impact. If your company is performing well, anticipate that each round will cost you between 15 percent and 30 percent of your equity. If things go sideways, capital could become much more expensive. To avoid giving away too much, demonstrate proof of concept. Show investors that you can execute and that customers will pay for your product. This will help to mitigate their risk and create significantly more value for your company.

Understand this: Every single little percentage point will make a big difference down the road.

Preferences. Investors typically have certain rights that supersede those of the entrepreneur. One example is preferences.

Preferences are special return scenarios that relate to what happens to the money when a given financial event occurs. For example, should you sell your company, investors may demand their principal be repaid first, after which the remaining money is divided by everyone else on a pro rata basis. Alternatively, an investor may have mandated that they receive two or three times their investment, then everyone else split the remainder. The lesson? Focus not only on how much equity you give away but also on the preferences built into investor agreements.

Control. Even if you own most of the equity in the company, you may not be in control of it. Many investors fight for contractual provisions that hand over to them the power to make decisions about certain aspects of the business. Be sure to understand how much control you are ceding.

Value. Beyond cold cash, what else does your potential investor bring to the table? Does he or she bring industry knowledge or operational knowledge? Will you gain someone skilled in team building or with contacts for strategic partners? Balance investors' overall value with the capital they bring to the table.

Raising capital is often a requirement to launch a new business, product, or service. It's hard work that takes time and dedication. The biggest reason why entrepreneurs fail to raise the funds they need is that they don't have a road map, so they waste time. They get in front of the wrong people. They say the wrong things. They overburden their target with too much information. When they finally do get an offer, they don't know what to look for and how to negotiate the best deal.

If you follow the steps in this chapter, you can steer clear of these problems and set yourself on a path toward success.

STAGE III.

COUNTDOWN AND BLASTOFF

The First Thirty Days of Business

CHAPTER 8.

GO TO MARKET!

I fear not the man who has practiced 10,000 kicks once, but I
fear the man who has practiced one kick 10,000 times.

—BRUCE LEE

Hammers and Nails

By this point you've spent several weeks moving forward with your
big idea, developing your business plan, refining your business
model, building a great team, and maybe even raising some capital.
You've got a lot of momentum behind you. Now it's time to get
your product or service ready to go to market. It's time to open your
doors, either physically or online. This is your moment for liftoff.

The most common mistake entrepreneurs make when launching something new into the market is trying to do too much at
once. The same is true of managers inside big organizations. I call
it *hammer-and-nail syndrome*.

Let's say I give you one hammer and one nail. Your job is to
hold the hammer in one hand and the nail in the other. All you

have to do is drive that nail into a piece of wood. That's it; just nail that one product or service. You may miss the first time or even the second, but eventually you'll nail it.

Now let's say I give you two hammers and two nails. You have a problem. Who is going to hold the nails? Let's say you find someone crazy enough to volunteer. Your job is to drive both nails at the same time into that piece of wood. Odds are you will miss again and again.

What if I give you three hammers and three nails? I think you get the point: This is exactly how most entrepreneurs launch their businesses. They simply try to do too much at once. They mistakenly believe that going to market with "more" is better.

It isn't. During your launch period, more means additional risk. More means unnecessary complexity. More means additional time to market and more capital required.

Below are some important things to remember as you prepare to take your product to market.

Don't try to build Rome in a day. I have a good friend who raised two million dollars in a very tough market to start a consumer Internet business. To have raised that much money so soon after the 2008 market collapse was amazing, and I congratulated him on the big win. He was ecstatic and told me he couldn't wait to get to work on the company's site.

In 2012 I ran into him again and asked how it was going. He sang the blues. They had launched their company a few months earlier but had already run out of money. How was that possible? When I asked, he talked about his big vision, how his company aimed to provide everything its target customer could possibly want to buy in the category. Its goal was to be a one-stop shop. He and his team had invested all their time and money building something big and comprehensive, confident their target customer wouldn't want to go anywhere else once their Web site was up and running.

After launch they discovered, to their surprise, that about 95 percent of their users used just *5 percent* of the site! Turn that around and it means that 95 percent of the time and money invested was effectively wasted.

Focus on one thing, the simplest thing. When launching, put all of your energy and focus into one product or feature at a time. It should not be the hardest thing; it should be the simplest, what we'll call the *minimum viable product* (MVP). The MVP provides the opportunity to learn the most about your customers, with the smallest amount of time, money, and effort invested. The MVP puts you in a position to go to market quickly, collect valuable feedback, and not waste time building things customers don't want. This strategy significantly mitigates your risk and helps avoid the trap my friend fell into of building a bloated product that nobody wants to use.

Follow the 85 percent rule: Good is good enough. Striving for perfection is the enemy of any product launch. As a rule of thumb, when the new business or product is 85 percent of the way there, you are ready to go. In my experience the level of effort required to reach 100 percent is not worth the additional time, money, and effort at this stage. You would be much better off shipping early, getting something into the market, and beginning to test.

Be great at collecting and learning from feedback. Once you have launched, listen to and learn from your users. Develop feedback loops that enable you to learn everything you possibly can. What do users like and dislike about the product? What features would they like to see added to enhance their experience? Which features don't work or generate little interest? Do whatever you have to do to engage with your users. That may include offering incentives, reaching out in social media, and generating outbound calls to learn more.

The hardest part of this process for many entrepreneurs is to be completely receptive to what customers tell them. Given your passion and all the time you have spent on the project, you may not want to hear negative feedback. You may be inclined to think the customer just doesn't get it. But feedback is the most valuable tool you have as an entrepreneur. So listen, consider, and use what you learn to iterate, improve, or even throw out some of what you have built or planned.

Avoid shiny-ball syndrome. As you start developing your minimum viable product, you must fight "feature creep" at every step. You, your team, your partners, and everyone else you share your vision with will have ideas about what should be added, and many of them will sound like good ideas at the time. More likely, though, they're distractions, shiny objects that draw your eye. Your job is to keep focused on one thing, to get it to market, and *then* to deliver the next single thing. By staying focused on one thing at a time, you can get to market quickly, learn a great deal from real customers about what you offer, and make changes. If your launch doesn't fly, you have significantly mitigated your risk.

Speaking of not working, what if the product falls down or is simply a bad product or a poor market fit? Kill it. In order to mitigate your personal and financial risk, choose to fail fast and shut it down. Big, fast failure is better than a long, slow, expensive death.

• • •

LAUNCH, LISTEN—AND LEARN

Focus: Launch your new products and services fast and launch them often, but always focus on one thing at a time. Don't start with the hardest thing but, preferably, the simplest thing, the *minimum viable product*.

. . . .

Listen: Launch quickly but, as you do so, develop feedback loops that enable you to *listen* to what your customers have to say.

. . . .

Learn: Make incremental changes and improvements based on feedback. Launch again, and continue the process of iteration, making it an ongoing part of your culture.

. . . .

Move On: Once you have really nailed that product, once you've found the right product/market fit and given your customers what they want, move on to the next one (that is, to the second hammer and the second nail). Remember, you can do everything you want, just not all at once.

Riches in Niches

My early career was spent in a broadcast world. I worked for divisions of media giants like CBS, NBC, and FOX. During that time I sold advertising to big global brands and marketed their products to the largest possible audience. The idea was to cast the widest possible net and see how many fish you could pull in. I believed in the power of mass marketing.

For the entrepreneur planning to launch, there's a problem with this model: too much marketing waste. Inevitably you'll spend a lot of money telling your story to the wrong people. That's not the way to build a business. You need to be razor sharp in cutting up the marketplace, making dead sure that every dollar spent on communicating to your target audience gets a good return on investment.

The good news is that that can be accomplished today in a way we couldn't do it twenty years ago. Instead of living in a world with a handful of television channels (like the world I grew up in), we now live in a world with literally millions of targeted ways to connect with your audience. You can find your audience on one of thousands of television stations that speak to your niche. You can pinpoint your market on the Internet and target it using Facebook or Twitter. In each case, today's consumers do for the entrepreneur what broadcasters couldn't years ago. They self-sort themselves into groups based on shared interests and desires. The key is to find your target and market to that audience very specifically.

Your task as an entrepreneur is to think in terms of an ideal customer—one person, one group—to whom you wish to sell your single, simple product. Develop a very specific profile, learning everything you can about your ideal consumers and what aspect of your product appeals to them. Determine what your target customers talk about and learn their manner of speaking, the lingo they use to speak to one another. Put yourself in their shoes. Know what they care about, their issues, and their concerns.

Once you have a very deep understanding of your customer, market your product or service to that very specific audience. Instead of broadcasting to a wide market, go narrow and go deep. There are riches in niches. The more you integrate yourself into that group (especially via sites like Facebook, Twitter, Tumblr, and LinkedIn), the faster word will spread about what you have to offer. If you talk to the right people at the right time in the right way, and you deliver a product they value, you will suddenly have an entire community telling your story and functioning as your marketing team. On the other hand, if you misfire, everyone will know—bad news travels fast.

I came to truly appreciate the power of targeting a deep and narrow niche when I worked on a project for a direct-marketing business. The owners had acquired a database that had more than fifteen million buyers of a certain type of product. They had names, physical addresses, e-mail addresses, and a lot of information about each buyer. Their initial plan was to use the list to market new products via e-mail.

When they started sending out marketing offers, they cast the widest possible net, sending the same offer for the same product to all fifteen million people. With that much distribution, how could they lose? They found, however, that a low percentage of people actually responded to the offers and a high percentage of their solicitations got dumped into spam filters. Many people simply weren't interested in hearing their offer.

We needed to change their approach. We brought in a data-analysis team and broke down the fifteen million names into ten groups that we called "buckets." In doing this profiling we learned that, although all the people were on this list because they bought a certain kind of product, their individual characteristics were very different. Not everyone was interested in the same products or wanted to be marketed to in the same way. We found we needed to sharpen our focus and tailor our message.

We made a critical decision to learn everything we could about one bucket at a time and developed very targeted products and services for each niche. That meant we ignored the rest of the millions of names in the database, because sheer volume wasn't what we were going after. We looked to isolate a particular kind of person. I would rather have fifteen thousand buyers I know are interested in my product than a database of fifteen million people who are not.

The original—and unsuccessful—offer had been for a weight-loss program. So we took a look at a segment of these people who had bought one product that could be loosely categorized as spiritual, such as Christian-themed products. Then we looked at the predominant gender of the people in that bucket, narrowed our age range, and chose one target demographic—women aged forty-five to fifty-five.

We kept adding filters: married; has children; empty nester; caretaker for a parent; pet owner. Now we were getting somewhere. All these qualities might make it sound like we were creating an overly narrow niche, but we ended up with more than a million names of people who met those exact criteria.

Then we went to work learning everything we could about our prototypical customer (we named her Christina). She was a fifty-year-old mom with grown kids who owned a dog and was caring for her parents. We joined Christina's online communities, found her on social media, and had real conversations with people like her. We learned what drove Christina and the kinds of products and services that she was interested in.

We developed just the right product, tailored to this ideal customer. In this case we built a spiritual program in the form of prayer books, newsletters, and audio and video recordings that touched on issues that were experienced by caregivers who also owned dogs. The response to the highly targeted campaign was amazing. Many Christinas bought the product, became part of the community, and referred other friends like themselves (and gave us their e-mail addresses). In one month the company recorded a much greater response, because we had connected with the market.

Here are a few suggestions on creating the perfect product/market fit:

Pick one very specific niche. Instead of casting a wide net, focus on solving one customer need at a time.

Develop your avatar. Create a very detailed representation of your targets. Who are they? What are their ages, genders, and locations? What do they care about? What do they read? Whom do they hang out with? What do they watch? Which products do they buy and where do they buy them?

Engage in conversations. Find the specific places they hang out (both in daily life and on the Internet). Join their communities. Learn what concerns them, what drives them, and what is under the surface emotionally that gets them to make decisions. Chime in when appropriate.

Crickets

You were convinced that when you built it, they would come. You knew in your gut that what your product offered was exactly what the market needed, that once you launched, people would flock to you in droves. But when you opened your doors, either literally or online, all you heard was the sound of *crickets*. Not footsteps, not voices, no pings, no cash-register noises. Just crickets.

You might have the best product around that no one has ever heard of. Or the few folks who have heard of it just don't know where to find you.

This is one of the problems I run into most with entrepreneurs. It occurs because of wishful thinking (*I know people will come!*), too little money to spend on marketing, or no workable strategy for driving traffic in the company's direction. It is just as common with intrapraneurs, who place exaggerated confidence in the past success of other launches or the strength of their company's brand.

A client recently came to me with a great idea for an online business. His product addressed an obvious need in the fitness business, and he had spent a year and $75,000 of his savings to build a beautiful Web site to sell it.

"How's business?" I asked, expecting a happy answer. "How many people are coming to your Web site? How many units have you sold?"

His answer: *None.*

He had almost no traffic to the Web site and few buyers exposed to his product. He felt like the business was doomed. To make matters worse, he had exhausted his cash resources building the product and promoting the launch.

But as I told my client, his business was not doomed. What he needed were partners. Not business partners but partnerships with other businesses, specifically ones that had a similar customer profile.

In nearly all the companies I've been involved with, a key to the successful distribution of our products and services has been the partnerships we established early on. By hitching your wagon to a bigger, more established business you can get a lot further faster, and with much less money out of pocket than by traveling the road alone. I've seen this strategy work firsthand. I've helped businesses grow from ideas to big brands—on the basis of sound partnering.

My first lesson in partnerships was with Quote.com. I was an early member of the consumer Internet business's launch team. In 1995 the company was one of the first to get permission from the stock exchanges to put stock quotes on the Internet. It helped create the market, define it, and was the leading brand in its category. Today, with hundreds of places to get stock quotes online, we take for granted how easy it is to find them. But back then it was state of the art. I remember giving a presentation to a team from the *Wall Street Journal* and they just about fell out of their chairs upon seeing real-time quotes delivered on big blue-chip stocks.

Quote.com had a great product in an exploding market, but we had to move fast to keep our first-mover advantage. At the beginning we had very little money to work with (I had to use my own frequent-flyer miles to buy airline tickets to go see a customer). Since we had a small marketing budget, we needed to find other ways to grow. We needed partners. Though we felt we had something valuable to offer them, we had to figure out a way to get in the door and structure a deal where both sides would win.

We approached sites with a similar target customer. These other companies wanted to create more awareness; they believed that offering more value would drive usage. They wanted applications that kept users on their sites rather than surfing off to explore other places on the Internet. And ultimately they wanted to find ways to monetize this traffic.

We offered to integrate our product into their Web site, giving users a reason to stay on their Web sites longer. We proposed co-branding the pages to create branding and awareness for both of us. Once we figured out how to monetize the pages together, we'd share revenue.

In just a few months we built a network linking us to over one hundred sites, some of which were among the largest consumer Web sites at the time. As a result, people began to see us everywhere.

We applied the lessons we learned about partnering to advertising as well. One of our key early advertising partners was Ameritrade. Its founder, billionaire Joe Ricketts, knew that different kinds of investors liked different kinds of brokerages, so he created four of them: Accutrade, K. Aufhauser & Co., Ceres Securities, and eBroker. Each one had a different marketing angle to appeal to a different kind of investor. Joe and his son Peter advertised Ameritrade sites on Quote.com because they knew if our customers wanted a quote, they were likely to have a brokerage account, making advertising with us a no-brainer. Everyone was a winner, and ultimately Quote.com became one of the largest advertising revenue–generating sites and number one in its category. The company eventually sold to Lycos. The whole experience serves as a great lesson in growing a company quickly with limited resources through partnerships.

I've watched the same model applied over and over in my career, with Sportsline USA and CBS, with Xoom.com and NBC, with Lycos and FOX Sports, and most recently with Smart Charter and Virgin. In each case a scrappy, early-stage venture with limited resources applied the same formula and created a win-win opportunity with partners to achieve its goals.

How do you apply partnerships to your business?

Decide what you need. What does your business need most at this stage? Capital, resources, access to potential customers, credibility, marketing and promotion?

Follow your target customers. Where do they spend their time? What businesses, Web sites, organizations, associations, or groups do they visit?

Create a win-win agreement and execute. Ask yourself, *How can I create a win for my partner? How can I make my internal champion look like a hero in his or her business? How can I get them so excited about this partnership opportunity that they think about it and prioritize it every single day?* To do this, find out what's most important to your prospect, what has to happen or how they know they are getting what they want. On the basis of feedback they give you, tailor your partnership ideas. Create revenue sharing where applicable that benefits both companies.

One final lesson on partnerships? I believe that businesses are bought and not sold. Many of the best financial exits are the result of businesses that started as partnerships and then grew into something more. Many of the people I have worked with who partnered early with the right businesses, followed through on what they said they would deliver, and built deep relationships throughout the group ultimately had the largest financial exits.

PARTNERSHIP PLANNING

How to prepare for and find a good partner:

Build a Good Business: A big partner will not make your business better. It will expose your flaws faster. You need to stand on your own two feet. Build a great product first.

Calibrate Your Needs: Determine what you want from a partnership: capital, resources, technology, marketing, distribution, or sales support?

Understand Their Needs: What problem can you solve for your partner? How can you make your internal champion look like a hero?

Sell What They Need: Focus the conversation on addressing your potential partners' needs rather than on what you think is cool about your product.

(continued on next page)

(continued from previous page)

Shop Around: Talk to as many potential partners as possible to be sure you find the right one.

· ·

Find an Internal Champion: Because smaller companies and new initiatives can get lost in the shuffle, you need an internal champion in the business you're partnering with to take owner-ship of your project and drive it internally. As an entrepreneur CEO, it's important for you to maintain a relationship with this person.

Crowdsource Your Sales Force

Sometimes the mirror takes awhile to clear so that we can see what's right in front of us.

Ever since college I've been surrounded by computers. I've worked and invested in several Internet companies. I've been an early adopter of new technologies. But there was one area in which I dragged my feet: I was late in embracing social media as a means of growing a business.

I was guarded with my privacy. I had very little spare time, and keeping up with Facebook, Twitter, LinkedIn, Tumblr, Pinterest, Google+, and everything else seemed like more to add to an al-ready full plate. But everything changed when I saw the potential value these networks had to offer when launching a new business.

I was advising a bootstrapping software company that had no marketing budget and very little money to hire salespeople. Since it couldn't afford to market its product and hit sales targets the traditional way, it turned its attention to social media.

When I taught sales training twenty years ago, I talked about finding target customers, identifying their needs, and demonstrating how a company's products met those needs. I'd go on about how to close the sale, provide excellent customer service, and in the end create raving fans who would share their experience with others. But here's what I learned.

The model has flipped. Today many of the most effective companies build fans *first,* customers *second.*

With fans coming first—this is the best part—you can effectively crowdsource your sales force. By executing this strategy you can build a virtual army made up of thousands of people talking about you and telling their friends to buy your product. And it costs you nothing. That's because you have the crowd passing along their experiences, giving personal referrals, and selling on your behalf. Your social-media sales force can be more effective than anyone you put on staff. People are much more likely to trust your brand and make a purchase based on a friend's referral than on the basis of anything you tell them.

I've also learned that social media can be an excellent tool for conducting market research, brand development, and product development and for getting direct feedback from customers.

So how do you crowdsource your sales force?

Pick one channel. Instead of trying to conquer multiple social-media channels at once, pick one platform to start with, whether it's Facebook, Twitter, LinkedIn, Tumblr, Pinterest, Google+, or another. Do that one well and don't worry about anything else. How do you choose which one? Find out where your customers spend their time. Go find them and engage.

Be authentic. When I first got started with social media, I made a big mistake. Everything I put out there was too highly produced. Whether it was a post, picture, or video, I thought it needed to look and feel perfect. But online, authenticity is everything.

Being you is what people want, and if you try to be someone else, they'll know. If what you put out comes off as scripted and highly produced, that feels to the customer like a violation of trust. So be yourself. Share and tweet and post the things that interest you. Don't work too hard to make everything perfect. Instead, focus on being raw, real, and relevant. And by the way, it's okay to be dorky.

Forget the gatekeeper. With social media you can connect with virtually anyone you want. That is an enormous shift in our ability to access others. There are no longer gatekeepers standing between you and the top businessmen, entertainers, and athletes in the world, because most of them manage and respond to their own social media accounts. If you would like to start a conversation with someone who might make a difference in your business, it can be very easy. Just send him or her a tweet.

Commit yourself to a daily hour of power. Getting started with social media is quick and easy. Opening an account costs nothing, and posting is free. In a few minutes you can be up and running. Within an hour you can reach out and be connected with friends, coworkers, and customers.

Spend one hour per day during your launch engaging with the community. That's it. In one hour a day, at zero cost, you can build an army. The potential payback is incalculable in terms of exposure and attention.

Monitor and protect your brand. Make sure to regularly frequent the sites, feeds, and pages that discuss your industry, product, or service. Look for posts that mention your company. Respond to comments and complaints, using them as opportunities to engage, build trust, grow your brand, and collect market research. If you listen carefully, you can get ahead of potential problems. And don't think you're exempt from this kind of vigilance if you're a big business. Today being big is meaningless if the customer's friend says the product sucks.

Invest in sound. If you are posting video or audio content, keep a couple things in mind. Even though the color, background, and production values may not be perfect, good sound is very important. Buy a lavalier microphone for quality sound and, whatever the source of your video, be sure there is enough light for people to see you. You don't need to spend a lot of money, but this is an example of one detail that you should invest in and pay close attention to.

Tell them how to reach you. Make it easy for your fans to get hold of you. If possible, have your Web address, e-mail address, phone number, or social-media handle somewhere on the video screen, and mention it in your post

Leverage social media as a research tool. I love fish. One of my favorite hobbies is building aquariums. I kind of fell into it; my daughters both wanted a pet, so we went to a local pet store and bought them each a goldfish.

I kept going back to that pet store, fascinated by the aquariums and the beautiful breeds of fish. It didn't take long before I decided to build my own aquarium, and before I knew it, I was building a second. Now I'm addicted, but I have a problem with the local pet stores: Their selection of fish is small. One day I grew so frustrated that I started thinking about opening up my own store. Not a pet store, a fish store. I needed more information, so I turned to social media.

First I went onto Facebook and searched for communities of people who shared the same interest. Next I went onto Twitter and starting following hashtags like #fish, #aquariums, #fishstores, and so on. There were a few people who were very active in these communities, and I approached them with questions: Is there a reason I can only find the same small number of fish breeds at the local stores? Do other people in the community have the same problem finding a good selection of fish? Has anyone been able to solve this problem and, if so, how did they do it? I found that when I asked these questions of the whole community, many of the people who responded had problems similar to mine. Maybe my fish-store idea had legs.

Then I asked my fellow online hobbyists the big question: If you could build the perfect fish store, what would it look like? To my surprise, the answer was not that the store would have the biggest variety of fish but that it would provide great customer service. What I learned was that many people dropped the hobby because they could not figure out how to build a good aquarium, maintain the right water balance, or even feed their fish the correct amount. As a result, their fish kept dying. The service at the existing stores was so poor that these people either got frustrated or felt embarrassed to ask for help, so they just dropped the hobby altogether.

I realized that if I provided better service, I would do more for the community. I also learned that customers would be more loyal to my store, stay with the hobby longer, and ultimately buy more stuff. In reaching out to online communities through social media, I saved a lot of money and time in getting my research done. Today that fish store is my pet project!

Your Buyer Blueprint

While teaching Tony Robbins's material twenty years ago, I learned that the biggest mistake salespeople make is selling the wrong thing. They push either what they think is most important about their product or what their boss has told them to sell. When the prospect says no to their pitch, they don't understand why. This happens because the seller never asked what the prospect wanted—nor did he understand the prospect's *buyer blueprint.*

Although I should have known better, I've fallen into this trap myself. One example was while I was at Virgin Charter. We had a very smart and educated team. We were confident that we understood the problems our customers wanted solved and how to solve them. With this confidence we created a product road map, listing the features planned for development and ranking them in the order we would build them. We had over a hundred features on our list and I had the sense we were really on the right track. Then, after spending lots of money building a Web site and going to market, we discovered that people just weren't using our service in the way we had believed they would.

Our team spent its time building features on the back end of our Web site, creating efficiencies, automating systems, and developing technologies that were necessary to enable buyers to complete a purchase and manage their trip details online. But customers spent their time on the front end of our Web site, doing searches and viewing profiles of all the available aircraft. When they wanted to make a purchase, most just picked up the phone, called, and asked our team to process the order.

I asked my team to go back out into the market. Our sales, product, and technical people gathered in rooms with customers.

We soon learned that some of the functions people had wanted most in the earliest versions of the product were neither in the current product nor among the top ten things to build in our product road map. Some were not even in our plan. Obviously, we had too many hammers—and not enough of the right ones.

The challenge is to create a solid buyer blueprint before you do anything else. You can create this by asking two very simple questions.

What is most important to you? Ask a customer this and many times the answer you will get is "I don't know." But try turning the answer around, responding with "I know you don't know, but if you did know, what would it be?" You'll find that that usually elicits useful answers, and the person will start listing the things he values most, perhaps without even realizing it. Take notes and, once the customer has downloaded his list, work with him to rank every item on the list in order, to identify which features are really most important to him. For example, if he could have this or that, which one would he choose? Continue to go back and rework and refine the answers.

The potential buyer may say, for example, that the top priority is that a food item taste good or, for a tech service, that it be easy to use. That's a start, but it's not all that you need to know. This leads you to the second question.

How do you know you are getting what you want? Nearly everyone forgets to ask this question, and it may be the most important one. Why? Because the definition of "good taste" or "easy to use" differs from person to person. We all have different rules or labels we attach to things. Your job is to find out not only what your prospects value but also the rules they have established for determining whether they are getting what they want. That makes follow-up questions essential.

How do you know it tastes good? Do you crave sweet or sour, crunchy or smooth? How do you know it's easy to use? Do you need to access it online? Would you require it on a mobile device?

With an early understanding of what your prospects want and how they know they are getting it, you will be able to build and sell products and services that match your buyers' blueprint and lead to big success for the business.

But remember this: Just because customers said they wanted something does not mean they will buy it once they have a chance to see it, use it, and interact with it. We found that out at Virgin Charter. What many customers told us they wanted before having access to the product was different from what they wanted once they had a chance to play with it. Sometimes buyers don't know what they want. It's not that they are trying to deceive you. It's that they can only know so much until they have a chance to experience what you have to offer. For that reason it is essential to do two things.

First, build one thing at a time rather than everything at once. That way, if customers start using your product and find they want something slightly different, you have not wasted valuable time and resources. Second, get customers to use the product as early as possible and collect as much feedback as you can (remember the MVP?). Then iterate, redeploy, and scale.

Constant interaction and communication with your users and ongoing reevaluations of your product and priorities are the best ways to keep moving forward in these crucial ninety days.

CHAPTER 9.

MAINTAINING YOUR ALTITUDE

Everybody's got a plan, until they've been hit.

—MIKE TYSON

The Ninety-Day Checkup

Now you've launched your business, and your hard work is starting to pay off. The company has begun to generate sales. Your customers are responding with great feedback. The market is buzzing about what you have to offer. You even brought home a good paycheck to deposit into the bank. Finally you have a chance to catch your breath.

The question is, what do you do next?

Take care of yourself. Your start-up and launch periods are a sprint. It's an intense time and you are forced to go all out, giving it everything you can. But you can't continue to go at that pace forever. You need to cycle in periods of rest to recharge your battery. This is a good time to take care of yourself and your health.

Are you keeping up with your exercise regimen, eating right, caught up on sleep? It is a good time to check in on relationships as well and reconnect with the people around you who made sacrifices so that you could pursue your dream.

Take inventory. Work closely with your team to take inventory of what you learned during your launch. Here's a great chance for the group to contribute, for all of you to learn together so you have the best opportunity to improve. What worked? What didn't go as planned? Did you focus too much energy on one area of your launch to the detriment of another? Did your supply lines, feedback loops, and financials perform the way you anticipated?

Remodel the business. Sometimes even a new house needs some remodeling, the plans adapted for what you didn't anticipate. The same is true in business. When you built your initial financial model, it was filled with assumptions. Now that you are in business, go back and study the new facts and figures against the model you used during your launch. Look at your income and expense projections, the time and resources invested, and the capital that was actually required to reach your goal.

Sometimes busy entrepreneurs fail to do this, but it's important to identify whether income, expenses, timing, or all of them were off and how all of these results will affect your need for capital going forward.

Reevaluate your team. Do you have the right players on your team? Did each individual perform the way he or she was supposed to? Do you need to make changes? Can you get the kind of performance you want with improved leadership and training? Can the people who got you this far take you where you need to go next?

Oftentimes entrepreneurs feel loyalty to the people who joined their business prelaunch and fought the early battles alongside them. But your job is to make sure this company always has the right people in the right jobs at the right times. You may need to cut the cord and make changes as your business matures.

Find opportunities to grow. Invest in learning activities to help grow and expand your team's capabilities. Decide how best to position the present unit to take the company forward. Ask the team what roadblocks they need removed to help improve results.

Consider adding new products and features. Work to strengthen products that have demonstrated success. Determine whether now is the right time to add new products or features based on customer feedback, instead of simply iterating and improving your current offering.

Plan for the future. Try to take a fresh look at your business. Update your goals, plan, and strategy using the inventory you took and counsel from the team. Evaluate your current and future cash needs and determine how you will meet those requirements. You should be in a great place to think strategically and move your business forward successfully.

Cash and Cardboard

The doors are opened to your new venture, and as far as you can tell you're doing everything right. You have customers coming in the door, and orders are flowing. You're beginning to feel like that crazy idea of yours might actually work!

Hold it right there. Before you begin to take it all for granted, I want you to hear about my friend Marty Metro.

Marty got his MBA from the University of Arizona at age twenty-three. He went into consulting, working at Andersen Consulting and then a boutique firm. Over time he became a supply-chain technology expert. When the dot-com boom turned to bust, Marty got laid off.

He decided to start his own company, selling recycled cardboard moving boxes. The idea came out of his own experience, since he refused on principle to pay the retail price for new boxes when he moved into a new house in Los Angeles. He would go around town grabbing used ones from liquor stores. It wasn't that he couldn't afford to buy the boxes. Marty just didn't like spending money on things he would use once and then throw out—and he figured he wasn't alone.

Leveraging his background in logistics, Marty started a company called Boomerang Boxes, selling used boxes for half the retail price. The business was eco-friendly and was written up in *Entrepreneur* magazine. Life was good.

Then he went broke.

"In three years I had spent every penny I had," says Marty. He had self-financed the business, and when the business needed more capital, he reached into his own pocket. He had burned through two lines of credit for $100,000 each. He had maxed out three credit cards at $35,000 apiece. The whole thing came crashing down.

Worst of all, his wife didn't know half the story—he hadn't told her he had actually invested more than she had agreed to. The crash of Boomerang Boxes changed their lives. They had to sell their BMW and Land Rover, and Marty drove around town in a dented 1986 delivery van; adding insult to injury, the van had the name "Boomerang Boxes" painted on the side. He got a day job as a telemarketer. Sitting in a cubicle all day, he was miserable working as a cog in someone else's system.

At night he kept trying to figure out where his business had gone wrong. He just couldn't understand why it seemed the more boxes he had sold, the worse things had gotten for the business.

Marty's problem was one I've seen again and again: *Growth kills cash.*

This may seem counterintuitive, but it is very easy to grow yourself out of business. Say you buy a product for five dollars and sell it for ten. That means the more orders you can get, the more profit you can make. Right? Not necessarily.

When you're small, you can afford to maintain a low level of inventory. If someone wants to buy a dozen widgets, you've got them on hand, and once they're gone, you'll order another dozen to replace them. But what happens when a customer comes back and orders five hundred widgets? You think, *Hey, that's great!* You go to your supplier, buy the widgets, and sell them to your customer. But here's the question that you should always ask yourself: *How am I going to finance this inventory?*

You may have enough cash on hand to buy the five hundred widgets from your supplier, but what if your customer says that he wants sixty-day terms? That means that to do the deal you tie up the cost of those widgets in your inventory. That diminishes your pool of working capital. If you don't have enough cash on hand to float your business until your customer pays you back, then your business may have to grind to a halt.

Back to Marty. Once he learned these lessons, he was convinced that if he could manage the cash flow, the box business would work. He decided to try again.

Hoping to interest people in funding a new version of his idea, he did a tour of banks and venture-capital companies to raise money. When they asked what had gone wrong the first time around, he explained how his growth had outpaced his cash requirements and what he would do differently this time around. Remember, showing potential investors your failures (given that you've learned from them) can be as helpful as touting a string of successes.

Not only did he raise the money, but Marty and his investors rethought their entire approach to the business. Instead of operating a retail store that sold one box at a time, the new model involved buying boxes by the tractor load from *Fortune* 1000 manufacturers for resale to other companies. In the past, big companies would just crush and recycle the cardboard boxes. Instead, Marty and his team sorted them, inspected them, and packaged them into moving kits for sale to regular folks or back to big businesses. The new model was akin to what dairies used to do with milk crates and bottles. When you got your milk from the milkman, you only bought the milk; the bottles went back to the dairy.

The new strategy worked. After succeeding in Los Angeles, Marty quickly replicated the new company, UsedCardboard Boxes.com, around the country.

The message from Marty's lesson is this: As your business starts to grow, don't forget to pay attention to two very important factors:

Growth eats cash. When you're launching a business and strapped for cash, big orders may do more harm than good, and a booming business can actually cannibalize itself. Before processing disproportionately larger orders, be sure you understand the impact, positive or negative, that fulfilling them could have on your business.

Invest from cash flow, not profits. When reinvesting in the company, base your decisions on cash flow, not profit. Have a clear understanding of what big capital expenses might be around the corner so that you don't run into a cash crunch.

Now that you know these lessons, don't be afraid to take a second bite at the apple if your strategies didn't work the first time around. If you have been part of a venture that went belly up, be open and honest with yourself about what went wrong. Seek the counsel of others, learn from your mistakes, and try to imagine how you would apply them to a new business.

Don't be afraid that investors will not be open to you the next time around. If you can clearly demonstrate what went wrong and the lessons you took away from the experience, you may be surprised at how fast people jump on board. The surest path to success is learning from failure.

Finally, Marty's experience reminds me of two practices we established early in this book: Separate your company's finances from your personal finances. And never hide deep losses from your loved one.

Kryptonite

What comic-book character best describes the entrepreneur? I think it would be Superman.

Entrepreneurs are the heroes of business. They start companies, execute tirelessly, and are on call twenty-four hours a day. In the early stages they put their stamp on everything, assuming responsibility for all decisions. They're the driving force behind all that gets done.

Just as in the Superman story, there's one thing that can knock the entrepreneur down. No, it's not kryptonite in our case—it's the failure to delegate.

If you want to grow your business and maximize its potential, it's important that you learn to hand over responsibility to others—the sooner, the better.

I have two female friends who started a chain of indoor playgrounds for kids. After operating the business for three years, they are generating plenty of cash and impressive profit margins for a retail business. Their goal is to grow the number of stores throughout their state, then take the business national. Will they get there?

I found that instead of focusing on growth, they still spend most of their time on basic administrative tasks. They have run into a trap that many entrepreneurs encounter; because they are so close to the business, they think they can do every job in the company better than anyone else. They can't seem to loosen their grip, and as a result their business has plateaued. Yet by simply handing over more administrative tasks (like answering the phone, taking orders, and cleaning), they could significantly increase the amount of time they spend thinking strategically about the business and growing it nationally.

The importance of delegation to growth was made clear in two conversations I recently had with clients.

In the first I spoke with a consultant who runs a good business and makes one hundred thousand dollars a year. I respect her skills. I asked her what she was planning to do that day. Her answer: "I need to schedule a bunch of phone calls and meetings and fill up my calendar. Then I need to go buy boxes and packing material and tape and bring them back to the office and pack some marketing materials for prospects. Then I need to go to the post office and stand in line and mail everything out." I asked her how long that would take. "All day," she said.

In the second conversation I asked a good friend (another consultant) about his day. He said, "I'll be out meeting with prospects and clients closing business in the morning, then I'm going on a fifty-mile bike ride to train for the Ironman triathlon." I asked how he could fit such time-consuming workouts into his schedule with all the bookings he needed to make, along with sending out presentation materials. "Why would I do that stuff?" he asked. "I leave it to someone else." He has a virtual assistant he pays one thousand dollars a month to handle all of his administrative tasks. His business makes more than one million dollars a year.

It's pretty clear to me that the difference between the consultant with the million-dollar business and the one with the hundred-thousand-dollar business boils down to delegation. The most successful business owners spend their time on what is most valuable to growing their business and delegate the rest to others. I'd suggest that my first client look into the following fixes.

Start by valuing your time. The fix isn't that hard: By handing over more administrative tasks (like answering the phone, taking orders, and cleaning), you can significantly increase the amount of time you have to work on the big picture. When is the right time to bring in this help? Today. You say, *How can I afford that?* Wrong question. Ask yourself instead, *How can I afford not to?* Your time is too valuable to waste.

You don't necessarily have to hire a full-time employee. Instead, bring on a virtual assistant and pay him or her by the hour. That person can handle scheduling, shipping, answering your phone, and responding to a lot of your e-mails for less than ten dollars an hour, perhaps working remotely from home. A small expenditure can give you the time you need to get in front of investors, prospects, and clients.

I think of it this way: You either have a ten-dollar-an-hour assistant or *you* are a ten-dollar-an-hour assistant. As an entrepreneur CEO, is that all your time is worth?

Train and trust employees to take on more responsibility. When you start a business, you are the head of every department in the company. You are responsible for every job function. But as you add people to your team, be sure to fire yourself from those positions and let them take over.

For example, say you hire a new head of sales. That's a good decision, one area of responsibility you can take off your list. Your new job is to let the person you have hired do her job. Get out of her way, redirecting the energy you had put into sales back into your role as entrepreneur CEO. Your superhuman energies are better invested focusing on what is required to grow. By delegating you will move your business further faster, with less effort.

DELEGATION DOS

Make a List of Everything You Do: For one week, make a list of everything you do (both business and personal). Provide as much detail as possible. Circle all the administrative tasks—reading e-mail, scheduling meetings, creating presentations, standing in line at the post office, returning phone calls—that don't require your level of attention and that you can hand off. Next, take a look at nonadministrative tasks and decide what can be handed off to other members of the team.

· ·

Same Systems, Platforms, and Tools: Get all your employees and assistants working on the same platforms and systems for e-mail, contacts, and calendars. Live in the cloud with shared folders, voice calling, and video calling. Make sure that your infrastructure is in place to help you grow and scale with little effort.

· ·

Refocus Your Energy: Get back to your role as entrepreneur CEO—or whatever position in the company suits you best. Spend your time there.

Maintaining your altitude can mean making a series of small tweaks to your processes—or a complete overhaul of your team, systems, and strategies. But you will not know what needs to be done unless you take the time to step back and take a hard look at how you're doing in these first days and weeks of your launch.

CHAPTER 10.

IF THINGS GO SIDEWAYS

When the glass looks half empty, don't pray for rain, head toward the river.

—GREG REID

Learning How to Crash

Being an entrepreneur is a lot like driving a race car. In launching a business you move very fast, avoiding obstacles all along the way. At times you may feel like you are about to lose control and crash, like you're heading head right toward the wall.

Last year my business partner and I decided to learn how to drive race cars. We headed to Las Vegas Motor Speedway to take a course on driving. The instructors helped us get familiar with our cars, then we strapped on our helmets. I was driving a brand new Ferrari 360 Modena, with the instructor in the passenger seat. Before completing my initial lap, I got my first big lesson.

Every driver starts with his or her head up and eyes focused way down the road. But as your speed increases, you feel a new type of pressure. It's all mental. The natural tendency for drivers is to narrow their focus, drop their eyes, and look down, right over the hood. As a result, you get tunnel vision, seeing every little bump in the track, every little piece of shredded tire. I found myself making lots of quick turns, tiny microadjustments.

On the racetrack tunnel vision can get you killed. Steering around lots of small bumps is one thing when you're going 25 miles per hour. But when you're traveling at speeds six times as fast? At 150 miles per hour, a sharp steering adjustment can cause your car to veer wildly. And you can miss what's literally down the road.

The same thing is true in a fast-growing business. No matter what your speed, you need to keep your eyes up and focused on the horizon. You can't lose sight of everything in front of you, including the goals you plan to achieve. Only with a larger view can you pick the best line to take around the corners. The little bumps in the road won't throw you off. Instead, the wider view will allow you to achieve a graceful kind of movement that enables you to stay in control and reach your goal.

Another thing they teach in racing school is how to crash. When you least expect it, the instructor tugs lightly on your steering wheel. Of course you panic, feeling like you will spin out of control. And what's the first thing that happens? Your head turns and your focus goes directly toward what you fear most: the wall. As a result, your arms just naturally follow, steering you toward a crash.

Having jerked your wheel toward disaster, the instructor does something else surprising: He puts his hand up against your helmet and pushes your focus back to the track. Where your head goes and your eyes go, your arms and the wheel follow. You're back on track again.

In business you'll speed into twists, turns, and hard corners. From time to time you may feel like you are losing control.

Remember: Your job is to keep your eyes up, focused on the horizon, without ever losing sight of the big picture.

Pedal to the metal, eyes on the horizon.

Panic Faster

Jack Welch, the legendary former CEO of General Electric, once offered a sound piece of advice to aspiring entrepreneurs. After he spoke to Entrepreneurs' Organization, the largest global network of its kind, somebody asked Welch what his number one piece of advice to an entrepreneur would be.

Jack's response? "Panic faster."

Entrepreneurs are by their very nature positive, confident, and sure of their business. These are all great qualities to have when promoting your venture, but when things don't happen as planned and the business begins to go sideways, those same traits can work against you.

Entrepreneurs can get caught up in their own story. They can get so busy reading their own press that they don't see what is really happening around them. That means they may not react to danger signs.

Out of fear of the unknown, entrepreneurs sometimes freeze or pretend things aren't happening. They put off the inevitable, not wanting to make hard decisions like letting people go or cutting expenditures. Their emotions interfere, and the result is inaction.

Then, before they know it, they're out of business and have lost everything.

So here's some advice on how to avoid that worst-case scenario.

Panic faster. As Jack Welch said, you can't stand around hoping or waiting for conditions to improve. When things start to go wrong in your business, drop everything and identify where your problems lie. Spend 20 percent of your time on the problem and 80 percent on the solution.

Control the dialogue. It's important, especially in small, early-stage environments, to control the message. By the time you are panicking, odds are the rest of the team is already there. Remember, in their day-to-day responsibilities your staff may be closer to market conditions, sales trends, and financial matters. Good times or bad, they may know what's going on before you do and be more willing to believe it faster than you are.

When big problems occur, you need to get out in front of them. Your team will be wondering three things: *What is going on? How does this affect me? Will I lose my job?* It's important to address these questions. It's just as important to redirect your team's focus away from the problem and on to devising solutions.

Get everyone's input. You have put a smart team in place. Leverage that talent to help you diagnose problems. Oftentimes employees have already identified them and have come up with solutions. They're just not encouraged or motivated to speak up. Team problem solving should be part of your culture. Get everyone involved, and encourage them to take ownership. Or would you prefer they sit around updating their résumés?

Leverage your network. Whether it's formal or informal, you should have a board of directors, a group of mentors, a team of experienced advisers and perhaps investors. You've consulted with them and asked their advice over the years because they are good at what they do. They know that young companies run into challenges. Don't think you're losing face by going to them in a difficult time and asking for advice. Don't be embarrassed or afraid to admit failings. They've been there and are here to help.

Experienced entrepreneurs are typically eager to lend a hand to a fellow business owner who sincerely asks for it. One of the most important lessons I have learned is the people who are the most successful are usually the most accessible.

Get in front of your customers. At times you will be far more effective getting out of the office and into the market. Get on a plane and go see your customers. Learn about their business and the challenges they may be facing. Perhaps they have a new need you can meet that is a pivot from your existing product or service.

Be transparent. If your business is having problems, it is important to be transparent with your customers. You want to control the dialogue and not let someone else, like a competitor, do it for you. By being up front you will create trust. You may even find that your customer can help you to design a solution.

Cut fast and cut deep. If you're really in trouble, either with your financials or in not having the right people on board to solve problems in a crisis, you may need to trim your team. Laying people off is one of the hardest jobs of an entrepreneur. You may feel not only like you have failed in managing your business but also that you've failed in providing for these people. But you can't let that paralyze you. You have a deeper responsibility to your partners, your investors, your family—and the rest of your employees. Sometimes you need to cut off the limb to save the patient. Your ultimate responsibility is to your business.

When you see that layoffs are inevitable, don't delay. Furthermore, never make these cuts small and incremental. Small cuts will kill your business because everyone will be wasting their time looking over their shoulders wondering if the ax will fall on them next, instead of staying focused on their work. Small cuts can paralyze an organization. When you have to cut, do it quickly and deeply. It's much better to reorganize, rebuild, and start hiring again under better circumstances.

Keep your eyes on the horizon. It's easy to get bogged down in the trenches, to be so muddy and distracted by the bullets flying overhead that you forget to survey the battlefield and take in the big picture. Doing so will help you find the right path to take you out of this tough period.

We're Out of Toilet Paper

Sometimes things go wrong. No matter how much passion and hard work you invest in a new venture, you may hit a point where everything is on the line. The future looks suddenly like it holds nothing but failure. So why not quit?

Being an entrepreneur can be very rewarding, but building a successful business is certainly not easy. When things get tough, really tough, your business will fail if you don't have a deep sense of purpose tied to it. Without a clear reason to stick it out, it's just too easy to walk away. My friend Dr. Kristi Funk and her husband, Andy, are a perfect example.

After completing medical school and a grueling five-year residency of eighty-hour weeks, Kristi looked forward to starting her surgical career. She was a resident at Virginia Mason Medical Center in Seattle when she was asked to join the Cedars-Sinai Breast Center in Los Angeles. She said no.

Breast surgery was still evolving as a specialty, and Kristi felt this new position wouldn't take full advantage of the surgical skills she had spent so many years developing, so she turned down the offer. But she soon realized the opportunity had less to do with performing surgery and much more to do with making a positive impact on the lives of many women. That surging sense of purpose changed her mind. She soon called back and accepted the job.

By the time Andy Funk entered her life, she had already become a well-known and respected breast-cancer surgeon. Although Andy was heir to the largest privately held German insurance-brokerage firm, which his family had begun more than a century earlier, Andy wanted to create his own path. At age nineteen he had forfeited his inheritance, made his way to California, started his first company, and promptly fallen $250,000 in debt. Instead of heading home, Andy had fought hard to turn things around. Within five years, he had sold three businesses and established Funk Ventures, a venture-capital firm, which had soon become a pioneer investing in socially responsible companies. He had overcome big odds to make it past his early disappointments; this experience would come in handy later.

As a result of his success as a venture capitalist, Andy became the youngest member of the board of governors of Cedars-Sinai Medical Center. Not long thereafter, Kristi and Andy met and married.

Kristi had by this point become one of Los Angeles's go-to breast-cancer doctors. Her high profile attracted much media attention and helped draw many patients to Cedars-Sinai. But this success meant longer hours for Kristi. She and Andy felt like they had no life to themselves, let alone time to build a family. To make matters worse, Cedars rejected her request to hire any additional support to reduce her workload. After Cedars refused to provide support, Kristi and Andy agreed that things needed to change, fast.

As a medical and wellness investor, Andy had been intrigued for some time by the thought of opening a comprehensive cancer facility with Kristi. The center, the first of its kind, would allow them not just to hire more doctors to reduce Kristi's workload but also to treat patients more effectively and with better technology. With their own facility they would have the opportunity to change tens of thousands of lives and have an even bigger impact on people. A strong purpose was born.

The plan came together quickly. They founded the Pink Lotus Breast Center and lined up their financing by recruiting other physicians who would partner with them. In the fall of 2008 they leased thousands of square feet in a Beverly Hills medical complex, which would soon cost them more than thirty thousand dollars per month. Within weeks of their signing the eight-year lease with personal guarantees, the U.S. economy went into a free fall and all of their financing disappeared. Lines of credit were closed, credit cards were canceled, and the physicians who had committed to join the venture and invest began to get cold feet. When they thought things couldn't get more complicated, they found out Kristi was pregnant—with *triplets*!

Having scraped together every penny they had, Kristi and Andy were determined to remain in their medical office and build their company. The Funks opened their facility in March 2009, on the day the Dow Jones hit its lowest point and just three months away from the impending birth of their triplets. Even though the business plan was built for a minimum of three surgeons, Kristi was the only doctor on staff. When the Funks couldn't pay rent— because they were quickly running out of cash—their landlord sat down with Andy and offered him two options: Get out of the suite or get sued. Andy and Kristi had no interest in leaving and continued believing that their vision would one day come to fruition.

Just as at Cedars, Kristi was working sixteen-hour days in order to try to make ends meet while Andy was trying to hold things together on the corporate and business front.

Without other surgeons in the practice, Kristi and Andy were able to maintain full ownership of the business, but they were also missing out on much-needed revenue. In addition, delayed payments from insurance companies meant cash often came in six to nine months after Kristi and Andy had to pay their own expenses. Cash flow soon became impossible for Andy to manage. Things were coming to a head.

Pretty soon they started running out of toilet paper at the office. When Kristi asked Andy why there was none, he didn't have the heart to tell her—they just couldn't afford to buy any.

It was clear that despite their best efforts, it just wasn't working. The children's arrival also meant the added cost of a bigger house and two nannies so that Kristi and Andy could work. With all the odds stacked against them, why not just close up shop, declare bankruptcy, and start over?

Well, it wasn't that simple for Kristi and Andy.

Although they faced incredible difficulties at this point in their business, they had a tremendous sense of *purpose*. They strongly believed that they were fighting for something that was much more important than their short-term problems.

Their persistence paid off. Despite sliding into more than two million dollars of debt, Kristi and Andy built a center with an improved approach to breast-cancer care. The business took off and began doubling in size each year. Kristi's continued television appearances on shows such as *Today, The View,* and *Dr. Oz* provided further visibility while breast-cancer survivor and Pink Lotus patient Sheryl Crow soon lent her name to the new Sheryl Crow Imaging Center at Pink Lotus. To top it off, General Electric selected Pink Lotus as the first treatment facility to introduce a revolutionary mammography technology to the country. New surgeons joined the team. The business started to recover losses. Even expansion became a reality.

After a few years on the brink of financial collapse, Pink Lotus was not just headed toward success—it would soon be regarded as one of the top breast-cancer treatment facilities in the world.

In May 2013 Angelina Jolie announced that she had undergone a double mastectomy as a preventative measure to decrease her risk of breast cancer. The multiple procedures were all performed at the Pink Lotus Breast Center under Kristi's diligent medical care.

Be it Angelina Jolie, Sheryl Crow, or one of the many thousands of other women who come to Pink Lotus for their breast health each year, Kristi and Andy are making a huge impact on many people's lives.

When I think of Kristi and Andy, one takeaway really stands out: Most entrepreneurs don't realize how close they are to breaking through just before they decide to quit. Their stories can help assure you that most people don't know how close they are to success the moment before they decide to quit.

If you are on the edge and thinking about shutting it down, here are a couple things to consider:

Get counsel from experienced entrepreneurs. Be open about what you are experiencing. The most successful people are usually the most willing to talk about their struggles and help others work through their own. It's kind of a rite of initiation into the world of the entrepreneurship, like the exchange of a secret handshake.

Join entrepreneur clubs and organizations. For added support join networking groups like the Entrepreneurs' Organization. The mission of such groups is to provide support to entrepreneurs just like you.

I've often found that one of the best ways to get through tough times is to talk to peers in these organizations. Many have already experienced the same problems you are wrestling with, and they want to help.

As Kristi and Andy demonstrated, if you have a strong enough reason *why* you are doing something, you will figure out *how* to make it happen. In order to live your dream, sometimes you need to combine that purpose with pigheaded determination and persistence.

Seventeen Days

Most entrepreneurs seem to have one response when others ask, "How's business?": "Everything is great!"

Many either believe or try to project that the business is making big headway, when nothing could be further from the truth.

Entrepreneurs need to be positive and project a certain image of strength. This is important to help attract investors, partners, and the best talent. That attitude inspires confidence and keeps family and loved ones at ease.

But what happens when things are not going as planned? What happens when the image you are trying to portray does not reflect what is actually happening inside the business?

Many entrepreneurs feel like they have no one to talk to. They don't want to go to their investors because they're afraid they will just be angry. They don't want to talk to their partners because they're afraid they will kill the deal. They don't want to go to their employees for fear they will start looking for new jobs. They don't want to involve their spouses because the emotional roller coaster may be too much. Last but not least, they don't want to admit to themselves that something may be wrong, very wrong.

Instinctively, what many entrepreneurs do is try to bury the news as a means of hiding from it. Meanwhile, the problems eat away at them and their business. That's certainly the wrong response.

All the answers you need may be just a phone call away.

As my friend Michelle Patterson says, "We don't want to show that we're vulnerable. But when we do, it leads to amazing things." She should know.

Since its founding three decades ago by then-governor George Deukmejian, the California Women's Conference has been bringing together women from all over the world to learn from one another and to grow. For most of that time the event was organized by the first lady of California, the governor's wife. But in 2012 Governor Jerry Brown's wife decided to discontinue the event.

Mrs. Brown's decision inspired Michelle. As an experienced producer of large-scale events, she decided to take the conference over full time, determined to keep it alive. She locked down a venue, built her team, developed a plan, and started to execute. Over the next few months she signed up thousands of attendees, brought in more than 250 exhibitors, and secured more than 150 speakers. Things were off to a great start.

As the event grew closer, two big things affected the business and its bank account. First, the team outsourced to handle sponsorships grossly inflated its projections. Second, the investor funding expected for the business also failed to materialize.

Michelle was deeply embarrassed. She was supposed to be an expert in putting on this kind of event, and now it was in jeopardy. Like many entrepreneurs, her first instinct was to tell no one, to remain positive on the outside while she struggled to figure how to make ends meet. But one day everything came to a head when a payment was due for the production, and Michelle had no money left. The organization was $1.8 million in the hole. Michelle had no idea how to find the cash she desperately needed.

As a result, the event was in danger of being canceled.

Michelle had just seventeen days to save it.

She broke the news to her husband first. She told him she was afraid that she was about to bankrupt the family. When she shared her real concerns, he responded with nothing but support. He told her, "After fifteen years of marriage I have watched you persevere in everything you do—and you would never forgive yourself if you canceled this event. There has to be a way. We are not the first people to be in this position. You know a lot of very successful business leaders. Why not ask for help?"

The next day Michelle made a phone call that changed her life. She reached out to the mayor of Long Beach. She also called the CEO of the convention center where the event was to be held. Michelle and the CEO met later that day, and she explained the event's financial problems. In response the CEO asked her one simple question.

"What's your favorite flavor of ice cream?"

"Strawberry," Michelle said.

With that, the CEO had strawberry ice cream brought into the office. He encouraged Michelle to take a deep breath. Then he said, "Let's dive in and tackle this together." She now had a partner to help take on this problem.

His response also renewed her confidence. Michelle realized that if she got her ego out of the way and opened up, people would respond in a way that would benefit the event. She went home and made a list of people whose counsel she thought might help her out of this mess. She called everyone on the list and the response she heard most was not "How could you do that?" or "How could you let that happen?" Instead, everyone wanted to know "Why didn't you tell me earlier?" or "How can I help?" Several confessed they had tackled similar challenges in their own careers.

Her network came out to help her get the business back on track. Two friends even postponed their honeymoon and moved into her house to help her dial for dollars and collaborate on the effort. Michelle realized that the more she helped people understand the real issues, the more candid she was, the more help they would provide. Soon she had an army behind her.

Together with this team of advisers, she executed. In seventeen days she went from being told to shut down and consider bankruptcy to reducing what was owed from $1.8 million to $150,000. The event took place and was a big success. So much so that its success led to the creation of the Women's Network and Women Network Day, a global holiday held every May celebrating women.

Michelle often reflects on what would have happened had she given up out of fear and let her ego get the best of her. Luckily, she didn't, and she learned a valuable lesson: When things go wrong, don't try to hide it. Instead of letting fear take hold, take action immediately. When you ask for help sincerely and honestly, you will get it.

It may not be easy, but here are some ways to, deliberately and with your eye on the horizon, dig yourself out of a business hole.

Illuminate. In the words of David Corbin, Sunshine is the best disinfectant. The more light you shine on a problem, the easier it is to tackle. Get it all out on the table. Don't hide anything. Once you discover the source of the problem, get right to finding a solution.

Ask for help. The truth is, we have all been there. Letting go of ego and asking for help is one of the greatest signs of leadership and strength. There will be times in your entrepreneurial life when you feel like you're at the end of your rope, just dangling there with nothing to grab onto. Everything you could possibly need may be just a phone call away.

If you must choose between your pride and saving your enterprise, that's no choice at all. Get over yourself, push down that ego, and ask for help with the problem. You'll be amazed at how eager people will be to come to your aid. There are people out there who have walked in your shoes. Find them and seek their counsel. Don't be afraid to open up about what you are experiencing. The more they know, the better they can help guide you out of a problem and into an opportunity.

No entrepreneur starts by thinking about what they will do if their big idea, the one that they've worked so hard on, goes sideways. But you need to keep these lessons in the back of your mind.

Nothing in life worth achieving ever comes easily. Sometimes you need to fight for your dream. Sometimes you need to let your sheer will and persistence carry you through. When things are tough, you don't always need to be out front if you have the heart to come from behind.

Remember, every single thing you need to turn that situation around is in you now or within your reach.

EPILOGUE

STEADY AS SHE GOES

Do the best you can until you know better. Then when you know better, do better.

—MAYA ANGELOU

Wing Walk

It was the day of our launch for Virgin Charter and I hadn't slept for twenty-four hours. The previous day Richard Branson had flown in from India, and we had done nearly fifty interviews, filmed an online news segment, and ended the afternoon on FOX News. A prelaunch party followed, with all the glitz and glam befitting his Virgin brand. I got back to my room with just enough time to shower before heading out to CNBC for the official launch of the business live in studio on *Squawk Box*.

The day started as one of the high points in my life, the culmination of a two-year journey. Still, I had all the anxiety of any business owner or product manager the day of his or her launch. I wanted my product to work and my team to perform. More than anything, though, I wanted to remember my three lines, the three talking points I had been told I needed to say on air.

Richard and I sat next to each other in the green room. He watched a small monitor while I rehearsed my talking points. Then he leaned in to me and said, "Scott, I've got a problem. I don't think you're doing a good enough job."

My stomach fell to the floor. You could say this was one of those low points on the emotional roller coaster.

He went on. "I don't think you're doing a good enough job getting promotion for this launch. I think I'm going to have to step in. Give me a few minutes to think about it."

A few minutes later Richard leaned back over and said, "Scott, I've got it. You and I are going to do a wing walk."

"We're going to do what?"

"A wing walk."

"What the hell is a wing walk?"

He said, "You're going to stand on one wing of an airplane, and I'm going to stand on the other wing. We'll each hold on to a rope with one hand and a Virgin banner with the other. Then we'll fly all over New York. We'll get more publicity than you ever imagined for your business. And don't worry. These planes are stunt planes. Your feet will be in metal boots attached to the wings. So if there's turbulence, you won't fall off."

He shared his idea with everyone in the room, and they all thought it was great.

I was too tired to think straight, but I knew enough to still be terrified.

Richard turned back to me and said, "Don't worry. I'll give you a diaper in case you need it!"

I sat back in silence. A couple minutes later he leaned in again. "Hey, Scott, I don't know if we'll be able to get the plane." I was totally relieved, again a new high. "So I have a backup plan."

"What's that?"

"You and I are going to go skydiving."

What?

"Richard, I've never done that before," I replied.

"That's the best part," he said. "We're going to go tandem. You'll be on my back, and we'll hold a Virgin sign. You're going to get more publicity for this launch than you've ever imagined."

"Richard, I'm not sure that's a good idea. Like I said, I've never done that before."

"Well, you know, here's the thing," he said. "I haven't either. So we'd better practice once before we jump out of the plane so I know where that thing is you have to pull to let the parachute out."

At this point I was so nervous I felt like I was going to get sick. I got up and started walking to the bathroom, but the CNBC stage manager summoned us.

Next thing I knew, we were out there in front of the cameras. The moment was supposed to be exhilarating, but I struggled to remember what I was supposed to say. In my earpiece I heard the producer say, "Fifteen seconds."

I looked over at Richard. He smiled at me. A twinkle in his eye seemed to say, "I can't wait for later."

We got back in the car after the interview, and I could still feel my heart pounding. Would I be wing walking or skydiving later this afternoon? Suddenly everyone in the car got quiet. Then Richard turned around, his face a big grin. He high-fived every-one in the car. He then looked at me, reached out to give me a high five, and said, "Scott, give me a high five. It was all just one big joke!"

The wing walk. The sky diving. He had just made it up.

"I just had to break you in," Richard said.

In a weird way, when I look back at Richard's prank, it wasn't any different from what entrepreneurs experience every day when launching their business, full of highs and lows, ups and downs (but usually not a wing walk!).

As you kick off your journey, it's important to bring your focus back to the task at hand, no matter what happens along the way.

The Circus and Start-ups

Wing walk? Well, maybe not. But launching a new business or product can be like a circus act. There are lots of distractions being thrown at you. Any one of them could take away your focus, leave you off balance, and knock you down. All of this puts you and your business at risk. I know this firsthand.

My friend Greg Reid has a long bucket list. You know, a list of things he wants to do before he "kicks the bucket." Last year one of those things he decided to take on was the flying trapeze. He asked if I'd like to join him.

I had no idea what I was in for. When I finally got a firsthand look at what I had to do, I was terrified.

Think about it. You're standing on a ledge thirty feet off the ground. To jump onto a swinging trapeze, you have to reach out and grab the idea . . . I mean, the swing. You leap and suddenly you're moving at three g's. That's right—three g's! You're launched.

Now you're flying through the air. You're holding on tight. But suddenly the thing gets tougher. If you don't keep moving forward, you lose momentum and you're at risk of falling. So you grab the next ring. Success! Things begin to get easier. You try a flip and you execute. You gain confidence but still, every time you climb the ladder to make that jump and push yourself further along, you still have those butterflies, standing thirty feet above the ground, looking at what is in front of you.

What I learned that day is that success is all about letting go. When I first saw those swinging bars and platforms, I thought, *No way am I doing that!* Some people can't get past the initial fear. They don't trust the net down below. They focus squarely on all the reasons they cannot succeed. Because that's what they focus on consistently, that's all they get out of life.

It's time for you to let go. It's time to let your momentum carry you forward.

Are you ready to fall or fly?

The day Greg and I trained for the circus, there were eight other people trying out the trapeze for the first time. We were the only ones to succeed. By the end of the day, we were doing backflips and catching other acrobats' hands midair. It wasn't because we were more skilled than anybody else. It was because we had the right mental attitude.

Letting go and jumping off may come more naturally to entrepreneurs than to most people. The experience is liberating, of course, as leaving your comfort zone can be a real boost for creativity. Taking flight—at launch, on a trapeze, whatever—can inspire you to think outside the box, to carry forward your momentum, to keep advancing your business. It just takes focus, practice, and a willingness to let go.

Just ask any of the more than four hundred billionaires in America or the roughly ten thousand people who have built fortunes of more than a hundred million dollars. Or a run-of-the-mill entrepreneur millionaire—I promise you, every one of those people can tell you they had to face the same fears you do. But they let go, and allowed their momentum to carry them forward. At times they fell, but they got back up again.

If they can do it, so can you.

Twenty Thousand Miles per Hour

Space flight has always fascinated me. The idea of a man sitting in a capsule and being propelled into space at over twenty thousand miles per hour is pretty incredible. The fact that astronauts can confront their fear and engage in something that appears so risky is amazing to me.

A few years ago I had a chance to meet a space-shuttle commander. I was able to ask him a question that I had wondered about for a very long time, concerning the moment in time where the ship is returning from space and reenters the Earth's atmosphere. During that time there's a communication blackout with the command center on Earth and the shuttle is surrounded by a three-thousand-degree ball of fire. When all that occurs, I asked, "Aren't you just freaking out?"

The commander said, more or less, "That part's a breeze." He explained that *positioning* the aircraft for reentry is what's really tricky. You're above the Earth, traveling at something like twenty thousand miles per hour—and you're flying upside down and backward. You need to flip the ship over and position the nose at an angle of approach of precisely 40 degrees. If you come in too fast or at the wrong angle, the ship could explode when it hits the atmosphere.

I asked him, "How do you do it?"

What I learned is that risk should not be all that risky.

In the case of the spaceship commander, he had NASA behind him. Thousands of people, decades of experience. A long history of success (and a few failures) from which to learn.

During those minutes of precise ship positioning and reentry silence, no one is focused on fear. They've all been trained by the best, including other space-shuttle flight commanders who have done it before. This isn't trial and error; it's modeling. Each person on the team knows his role. They've practiced for years. They understand how to navigate through challenges. They execute together flawlessly.

In your business you need to do the same to mitigate what could go wrong and speed up success. Find and study role models to help eliminate risk from your business and to help save you valuable time and money. Learn what others have done to achieve the outcome you want. Study their specific beliefs, their strategies, and the exact order in which they did things. Then do the same things.

TALKING TO YOURSELF

Now matter what life throws your way, you can choose how to respond to it.

. . . .

Control Your Inner Dialogue: In every situation your brain asks two important questions: *What does this mean?* and *What should I do?* The questions you ask to evaluate the situation will determine what you focus on. What you focus on will determine how you feel. How you feel will determine how you behave. How you behave will have a tremendous impact on your business.

. . . .

Break the Pattern: If you catch yourself asking negative and disempowering questions—or if you find yourself caught in a terrible loop—break that pattern and insert questions that get you to analyze the situation in new, empowering ways.

. . . .

Make This a Habit: It will change your life forever. Before you know it, you'll believe that the universe is conspiring on your behalf!

Keep Your Eyes on the Horizon

We're coming full circle. Remember that the number one key to success is maintaining your focus. That means controlling your inner dialogue as you keep your eyes on the horizon. In doing so, you'll be able to anticipate, prepare for, and plan for whatever may be in your path and then steer gracefully around it.

This is not easy to do. It takes a lot of practice and hard work. It's like building a muscle. But if you focus on getting better in this one area of your life, each and every day, you will get stronger. You will be better able to manage through the ups and downs of entrepreneurship successfully.

No matter what life throws at you and no matter how high that wall looks, you need to take it all on. You'll find it helps to manage your focus by asking empowering questions that drive your energy toward a solution.

As a Lakers fan, some of my fondest memories are of watching the Lakers "Showtime" era in the eighties. My favorite player then—and one of my personal heroes now—was Earvin "Magic" Johnson. On the basketball court he lived up to his nickname because of his focus, his ability to concentrate on the objective at hand. He was always in the zone, in the flow of things. He won five championships and gained a place in the NBA Hall of Fame as one of the greatest to ever play the game.

Magic performed not only on the court but in business as well. Even before he retired from the game he founded Magic Johnson Enterprises, planning for what came next. His first big investment was a partnership with businessman Earl Graves Jr. when, in 1990, they bought a Pepsi-Cola distributorship. Magic got involved in movie theaters and inner-city redevelopment projects. In 1998 he partnered with Starbucks to create a company called Urban Coffee Opportunities, opening franchises in inner-city neighborhoods and building out more than a hundred locations before selling them back to Starbucks in 2010 for what's believed to be more than fifty million dollars.

Johnson is also a lead investor in the $1 billion Canyon Johnson real estate fund and the $500 million Yucaipa Johnson private equity fund. He owned a piece of the Lakers for many years and joined with Guggenheim Partners in its $2 billion acquisition of the Los Angeles Dodgers. He's now working on a venture to bring an NFL team back to Los Angeles.

Some people may say he was just lucky or born with that talent. But Magic Johnson is somebody who has jumped over more than his share of barriers.

In 1991 I was promoting a Tony Robbins event in Houston, Texas. The Lakers were scheduled to play the Rockets. There were a lot of fans on my team, so we decided to go to the game and got great seats right behind the Lakers bench. But Magic was missing from the action that day. His absence seemed strange because we hadn't heard about any kind of injury that would keep him out of the lineup.

Then, on November 7, 1991, I saw the breaking news on television: Magic Johnson was HIV positive. The first thing I thought was, *Will Magic survive?* But that was not Magic's first reaction.

Longtime Lakers trainer Gary Vitti recalls that when Magic first learned the news, he said, "Well, God gave this to the right person, because I'm going to do something with it." And he has. He used his diagnosis as an opportunity to educate and inspire millions of people around the world. He gave hope to people who at the time seemed without hope, creating the Magic Johnson Foundation to help combat HIV. He became the symbol not only for survival but also for successful treatment.

How does this relate to your launch? By controlling his inner dialogue and asking a different set of questions from the ones most people would have asked in the same circumstance, Magic was able to keep himself in the strongest possible position to steer through the medical challenges he faced. Even in the worst of circumstances, consciously or subconsciously, he used this skill to maintain his focus and move his life forward in a positive direction.

If Magic could overcome a challenge like this, I know all of us can overcome the things we battle every day in our businesses by maintaining our focus, controlling our inner dialogue, and keeping our eyes up on the horizon.

Fill Your Cup First

Some people get it backward. I have worked with many entrepreneurs whose primary driver for starting a business was to create a vehicle for serving others or facilitating a specific social change. These are noble purposes.

Here's the problem. Many people who start new ventures with these goals in mind place too much of their focus on the social aspect of their venture and don't spend enough time building a fundamentally sound business.

While I admire their passion, I also know that focusing on giving first and creating a sustainable business second usually leads to failure. That's because without creating a solid business that generates cash, these entrepreneurs are more likely to go out of business. As a result, they are not able to have the long-term impact they had hoped to achieve.

If your goal is to create a platform that gives back, I think that's awesome. But make sure you have your priorities in order. First create a fundamentally sound business, one that creates profits and generates sustainable cash flow. Once you have reached that threshold, use what you choose to give back.

Best-selling author and speaker Les Brown puts it well. He likes to say, "Fill your cup first. Let what spills over feed others." If you take this approach, you will create not only stability for yourself but also abundance that can be shared with the world.

Now, if you've reached a point where you can afford to give back but are looking for a cause, I'd suggest this: Give to other entrepreneurs.

When you're in orbit and you look down and see someone who has taken a shot, who may be struggling, reach out and give them a hand. Maybe it's financially to help them get through a tough period. Maybe it's by offering advice or being a sounding board.

When given the opportunity, invest in new businesses. Serve on boards. Assist entrepreneurs in launching new and innovative products and services. After all, it's these dreamers who keep our economy moving, who create jobs and growth.

Use your position to fuel the entrepreneurial spirit that is the heart and soul of America. Be there to support others who will be going down a road you have already traveled. You know they must take their own wing walks, try flying a trapeze, and race around tough corners. If you can keep them from falling, from hitting the wall, you'll be giving back in a way that can benefit all of us.

ACKNOWLEDGMENTS

There are so many people I would like to thank for their contribution to this book. First, to Demetri Boutris and Bruce Perlmutter, who got this whole process started. This would have never happened without the hard work of Nena Madonia and the amazing team at Dupree/Miller or without the support and encouragement of Adrian Zackheim, Natalie Horbachevsky, and the rest of the team at Portfolio/Penguin. Special thanks go out to Chris Helman for his valuable insights along the way. Finally, thank you to Gary Goldstein, Ron Klein, and Raoul Davis for all of their guidance.

On a personal note:

I would like to thank my mother for being so incredibly supportive. For going on this ride with me for the past twenty-five years. You taught me the value of persistence, hard work, and always looking at the "bright side" of a situation, no matter how hard it might have seemed in the moment. Thank you for always believing in me.

To Big D, thanks for being the rock in our family and having the patience to sit with me, on so many long nights, to talk about business. You were the greatest influence on my career when I was getting started.

To my sister Ashley and brother Shane, you have always been there for me. You have helped me in so many ways on more than one occasion. Thank you!

To Dad, I'll never forget all the football, baseball, and basketball memories growing up. What a great dad.

To Steve Rosendorf and Debbie Nessen, wow, did I get lucky! I hit the jackpot!

To Julie and Jay Don Johnson, many more great years together.

To Dan Clivner and Steve Cochran, you are family. You will never know how much I appreciate your support.

To Greg and Allyn Reid, you are the true definition of friendship.

Additional thanks to those who gave me a shot somewhere along the way: Richard Branson, Gabriel Baldinucci, Dan Porter, Stephen Murphy, Jon Peachey, Christine Choi, Julie Cottineau, Nirmal Saverimuttu, Ron Garret, Steve Chien, Dena Cook, Brooke Hammerling, Tony Robbins, Mike Hutchison, Ross Levinsohn, Chris Cottle, Jeff Tang, Jed Savage, Jason Port, Chris Kitze, Laurant Massa, Russell Hyzen, Kelly Perdew, Mark Moses. To the team at Virgin Charter for giving it their all.

RESOURCES

Recommended Reading

Unlimited Power, Anthony Robbins

Stickability, Greg S. Reid

Wooden: A Lifetime of Observations On and Off the Court,
  John Wooden

As a Man Thinketh, James Allen

Losing My Virginity, Richard Branson

Crossing the Chasm, Geoffrey A. Moore

Do You!, Russell Simmons

The Lean Startup, Eric Ries

Secrets of the Millionaire Mind, T. Harv Eker

The Mackay MBA of Selling in the Real World, Harvey Mackay

The Art of the Start, Guy Kawasaki

Crush It!, Gary Vaynerchuck

Seven Spiritual Laws of Success, Deepak Chopra

The Innovator's Dilemma, Clayton M. Christensen

Think and Grow Rich, Napoleon Hill

Permission Marketing, Seth Godin

Chicken Soup for the Soul, Jack Canfield and Mark Victor
  Hansen

Rework, Jason Fried and David Heinemeier Hansson

Zen and the Art of Happiness, Chris Prentiss

Tribal Leadership, Dave Logan, John King, and Halee Fischer-Wright

Do More Faster, David Cohen and Brad Feld

Delivering Happiness, Tony Hsieh

Program to Purchase or Attend

Business Mastery, Tony Robbins & Chet Holmes

Blogs to Follow

Seth Godin: sethgodin.typepad.com

TED: ted.com/talks

Vaynerchuk (Gary Vaynerchuk): garyvaynerchuk.com

This Week in Venture Capital: youtube.com/show/thisweek inventurecapital

Blog Maverick (Mark Cuban): blogmaverick.com

Chris Brogan: http://www.chrisbrogan.com/

Copyblogger: http://www.copyblogger.com/

INDEX

3-14